Building
the
Reading
Brain, PreK-3

PATRICIA WOLFE
PAMELA NEVILLS

Building the Reading Brain, PreK-3

CORWIN PRESS
A Sage Publications Company
Thousand Oaks, California

For information:

Corwin Press
A Sage Publications Company
2455 Teller Road
Thousand Oaks, California 91320
www.corwinpress.com

Sage Publications Ltd.
1 Oliver's Yard
55 City Road
London, EC1Y 1SP
United Kingdom

Sage Publications India Pvt. Ltd.
B-42, Panchsheel Enclave
Post Box 4109
New Delhi 110 017 India

Printed in the United States of America

Library of Congress Cataloging-in-Publication Data

A catalog record for this book is available from the Library of Congress.

This book is printed on acid-free paper.

04   05   06   07   08   10   9   8   7   6   5   4   3   2

Acquisitions Editor:	Jean Ward
Production Editor:	Julia Parnell
Typesetter:	C&M Digitals (P) Ltd.
Proofreader:	Penny Sippel
Indexer:	Kay Dusheck
Cover Designer:	Tracy E. Miller
Production Artist:	Lisa Miller
Illustrator:	David Stockman

Contents

Acknowledgments

I am indebted to the many researchers and authors who have spent their careers studying the processes that lead to competent readers. The seminal work of Marilyn Jager Adams is essential for anyone attempting to understand the vast amount of research that has taken place over the past three decades. Marie Clay's studies and the resulting Reading Recovery program have given us invaluable information regarding the teaching of reading, especially to those who experience difficulty. The brain-imaging work of Sally Shaywitz and Susan Bookheimer has provided us with an exciting new neurological perspective, an ability to see what is happening in the brain as a person reads.

Kay Soper, reading specialist in the Napa Valley Unified School District, graciously read several chapters of the book and provided excellent feedback. My good friend and colleague, Robert Sylwester, also read the book and gave his usual succinct and helpful suggestions.

—Pat Wolfe

Many contributed to the messages contained within these pages. I was encouraged by colleagues at the West End SELPA, San Bernardino County, California, who expect all children will make appropriate academic gains, especially in reading. Teaching struggling readers through a reading academy in the Central School District provided real-time classroom issues, challenges, and limitations. Teaching friends Royene Higashi and Pat Holt contributed examples of classroom experiences on a regular basis, along with special educators in the Alta Loma School District, who helped take research review to a practical level. I am grateful to colleagues Terry Thatcher and Ann Hagmaier for their willingness to read and provide feedback.

Current, research-tested information comes from an avid reader and active thinker, Kevin Feldman, Sonoma County Office of Education, via his massive e-mail distribution database. The benefit Kevin imparts to educators is immeasurable, and his messages provided many directions to be followed as this work developed. Grandsons Nathan and Neil gave willingly of their time for experiment and to provide experience with how reading happens in young minds. A word of gratitude also goes to my husband, Neil Nevills, who listened and understood the dedication of time that is required to produce a manuscript. The book was enhanced through painstaking review, questions, and suggestions from acquisitions editor, Jean Ward, and the persistence and patience of developmental editor, Tish Davidson. A special word of thanks to my co-author and friend, who said to me about 10 years ago, "Pam, you really need to start reading about how the brain is involved in learning."

—Pamela Nevills

Corwin Press would like to thank the following reviewers for their contributions:

Diane Barone
Professor, College of Education
University of Nevada, Reno
Reno, Nevada

Yvette Jackson, Ed.D.
Executive Director
National Urban Alliance
New York, New York

Donna Ogle
Professor, College of Education
National-Louis University
Evanston, Illinois

Robert Sylwester
Emeritus Professor of Education
University of Oregon
Eugene, Oregon

About the Authors

Patricia Wolfe is an independent consultant who speaks to educators in schools across the United States and in international schools. Her professional background includes public school teaching at all levels, staff development trainer for the Upland School District, Director of Instruction for the Napa County Office of Education, and a lead trainer for the International Principal Training Center in Rome and London. Her staff development experience includes workshops in Madeline Hunter's Elements of Effective Teaching and Clinical Supervision, Anthony Gregorc's Mind Styles, Carolyn Evertson's Classroom Management and Organization, and Peer Coaching. She has been featured in a number of videotape productions and satellite broadcasts.

Wolfe's major interest over the past 15 years has centered on the educational implications and applications of current neuroscience, cognitive science, and educational research for teaching and learning. She can be reached at Mind Matters, Inc., 555 Randolph Street, Napa, CA 94559, Phone and Fax: (707) 226-1777, Web site: www.patwolfe.com.

Pamela Nevills is first and foremost a teacher, working with learners from multiages—primary grades through post graduate students. Her undergraduate work at California State University, Los Angeles, was furthered by masters and doctorate degrees from the University of La Verne. She held teaching, staff development, and administrative positions and serves on and has been honored by local and state advisory committees. She is a national and international speaker and consultant on topics that include Brain Development from Birth Through Adulthood, The Brain and Reading, School Designs for All Readers, Adult Learners, and Administrative Leadership Skills.

Writing is a recent addition to Pam's work. She is published through the state of California, the Journal of Staff Development, and she regularly contributes to organizational newsletters. Her passion about the brain and reading developed from a childhood love affair with books, grandchildren who are emergent readers, and encouragement from a dear friend, Pat Wolfe. Pamela can be reached at 1619 Tecalote Drive, Fallbrook, CA 92028; phone (909) 894-2100; e-mail address: panevills@earthlink.net.

Introduction

All parents want their children to succeed in school and to thrive in the world outside of school. All educators share that same hope for the children they teach. In today's world learning to read well is a key to the future success of these children. Not only is reading fluently and with comprehension by third grade a legislated priority, it is an ethical and professional imperative.

Our purpose in writing this book is to bring to the field of developing literacy a focus that has become possible only through recent developments in neuroscience. We have set ourselves the ambitious task of aligning new developments in neuroscience that help illuminate the reading process and current reading theory and practice. It is our hope that this work will provide parents and educators with a better understanding of the ways that they can help to leverage reading success.

First, we look at the role of parents and caregivers as they work together with young children to build that most ancient and fundamental human communication bridge—spoken language. We offer parents and caregivers ways to build on children's natural proclivity for speech, and to begin to nurture them in an appreciation and understanding of language, print, and books to support the process whereby children move from spoken language to understanding symbolic written language.

Next, by examining the neurobiology of language and the scaffolding it provides for the cognitive processes of reading, we hope to help educators use the best of what we know of how the brain learns and merge it with what we know from reading experts about the best reading instructional practices. Throughout, our specific focus is the connection between brain research, language, and reading instruction. For that reason, the work of one researcher, Sally Shaywitz, is cited with particular frequency, as Shaywitz's work is at the forward edge of reported research based on images of brains as they read or struggle to do so.

Looking through the new clarifying lens of brain imaging, we see how some children experience greater challenge in becoming readers and look at possible appropriate interventions for these children. From what we know of the brain, we have drawn conclusions about applications for classroom instructional decisions and practices that are in line with how the brain learns, how teachers can help to build the reading brain, and how they can differentiate instruction for struggling readers.

It is our great hope that this book will benefit all of those people who work to ensure reading success: parents and families, caregivers for young children, nursery school teachers, pre-service and in-service primary teachers, faculty study groups, staff developers, literacy coaches, and school leaders. To facilitate reflection, discussion, and application of the ideas that we offer, we have included reflection prompts at the end of each chapter.

The chapters of this book are arranged to look chronologically at language and reading development. Parents, early caregivers, and teachers may choose to begin reading where they expect immediate application to their situations. However, we would like to note that chapter 2 with its overview of how the brain processes language and reading, is particularly important as it provides a foundation for the rest of the book.

Chapter 1 provides an introduction to the reading process and explains why reading is an "unnatural" act and discusses the factors which influence whether or not children will become fluent readers. An explanation of the various components of the reading act with an explanation of terms such as phonemic awareness and phonological processing comprise the remainder of the chapter. In chapter 2, the authors explore the neurological processes involved in learning to read. The language pathway–which is hardwired in the brain at birth–provides the foundation for building the reading pathway. However in some children problems occur which prevent or hinder their brains from making the transition from language to reading. This chapter concludes with a discussion of the biological and environmental causes of reading difficulties.

Because the brain uses the innate language pathway to learn to read, the development of language is an essential precursor to reading. Chapter 3 looks at how parents and caregivers can encourage and enhance oral language in their children from birth to age 3. It explains why reading to children and teaching them nursery rhymes helps to build the brain structures children will need in order to read. Chapter 4 continues this discussion with a focus on emergent literacy in preschool children. Discussed are developmentally appropriate activities and methods for continuing oral language development.

As children enter school requirements for learning become structured and complex. Children are expected to be able to focus their attention on tasks that involve interpretation and production of symbols that represent our oral language system. In Chapter 5 preparation for school tasks are identified as priming skills. Beyond the skill of attending the chapter provides a description of memory systems and concludes with rationale and practical activities to maintain student motivation, concentration and to develop organizational skills as work for the brain. The kindergarten and first grade child are the focus of Chapter 6. Here the authors identify phonological processes and manipulations to reshape neural pathways in the brain for the oral reading process. Teaching issues for phonics, spelling, and writing are discussed for children to develop a repository of words for long-term memory storage and decoding automaticity.

Primary-aged children's brains are malleable and plastic; they are more open to learning than at any other time during formal education. When a child is not successful with school tasks for reading early intervention is critical. Chapter 7 identifies assessment and intervention issues for struggling readers. Comprehension and vocabulary development with a focus on second grade children forms the essence of Chapter 8. The authors provide a discussion of what teachers can do to help children build extensive vocabularies, expand informational chunks for memory and form connections among thoughts and concepts in novel and exciting ways.

Reading competency develops when children experience sequential, planned instruction and are exposed to lots of books to capture their attention. Chapter 9 pulls all reading skills together with a focus on fluency. Fluency, as defined in this chapter, is observed when a child is able to read out loud with automaticity. Fluent readers demonstrate speed, accuracy, and proper expression while they concentrate on meaning. Building the reading brain, a construction process for the school years, is discussed in Chapter 10. A twelve point list that results from the book's content provides a conclusive summary. Finally, it is acknowledged that it takes talented teachers, who understand how children learn to read, to orchestrate a delicate balance of instruction, student engagement, conversation, and reading practice so that their students are able to read with a natural amount of effort and with obvious enjoyment.

On the Nature of Reading

1

THE IMPORTANCE OF LEARNING TO READ

Literacy is a relatively recent addition to human culture. Humans have used oral language for perhaps 4 million years, but the ability to represent the sounds of language by written symbols has been around for only 4,000 to 5,000 years. Until the twentieth century, nearly every human on earth was illiterate. However, the expectation in today's society is that 100 percent of the population will be able to read and comprehend. We live in a society where the development of reading skills serves as the primary foundation for all school-based learning. Those who do not read well find their opportunities for academic and occupational success are severely limited. Although the expectation that all children will read and comprehend is understandable, we are a long way from reaching this goal.

According to the National Center for Educational Statistics (1998), 38 percent of fourth graders in the United States cannot read at a basic level. This means they cannot read and understand a short paragraph of the type found in a simple children's book (Lyon, 2001). A child who is not at least a modestly skilled reader by the end of third grade is unlikely to be a skilled reader in high school. In fact, research has shown that we can predict, with reasonable accuracy, students' future academic success by their reading level at the end of third grade (Slavin, 1994).

> *Literacy is a relatively recent addition to human culture.*

Lack of skill in reading also has a potent effect in other areas. Surveys of adolescents and young adults with criminal records indicate that at least half have reading difficulties. Some states actually predict their future need for prisons by fourth-grade reading failure rates (Lyon, 2001). Similarly, nearly 50 percent of youths with a history of substance abuse have reading difficulties (National Institute of Child Health and Human Development, 2000). An increasing proportion of children are labeled "learning disabled," with most being identified because of difficulties in learning to read. There are those who believe the special education population in our schools could be reduced significantly by giving more attention to early interventions designed to prevent reading problems (Kotulak, 1996).

> *A child who is not at least a modestly skilled reader by the end of third grade is unlikely to be a skilled reader in high school.*

WHY LEARNING TO READ IS SO DIFFICULT

Our biological destiny is speaking, not reading. Speaking is a natural development; reading is an unnatural act. This means that almost every child will master speech just by spending time with people who already speak. Spoken language has become "hardwired" in the brain with structures built specifically for language. There are no naturally designated neural mechanisms for reading, however, so the brain must co-opt structures designed for other purposes. As the eye chases the words in a sentence across the page, the brain must continuously use neural systems designed by nature for entirely different tasks, such as looking for food or predators.

Even though reading is an acquired skill and not a natural process, most people do become fluent readers, but not without a lot of work. Learning to read is a long, gradual process that begins in infancy. Basic competency usually is not reached until middle childhood. As reading researcher Sally Shaywitz, professor and director of the Yale Center for Learning and Attention, states, "Reading is the most complex of human functions" (Shaywitz, 2003).

> *Speaking is a natural development; reading is an unnatural act.*

Reading in any language poses a challenge, but reading in English is particularly difficult. For example, some language systems, such as the Japanese *katakana*, are based on a system where each syllable is represented by a written symbol. When these symbols are learned, the child can read with relative ease (Snow, Burns, & Griffins, 1998). Spoken English, on the other hand, has approximately 5,000 different possible syllables. Written English uses a system of letters—an alphabet—to make up a spoken syllable. A letter alone does not refer to anything. It must be combined with other letters to represent a meaningful unit or syllable. The child must learn this complex alphabetic system in order to be able to decipher written words.

Reading in English is further complicated by its orthography—the spelling of words. In some languages, such as Spanish, one letter has one sound. In English, one letter can represent several different sounds, depending on its placement in the word. It is understandably difficult to figure out the sound-symbol relationship when the sound of a particular letter changes in words that have the same root but different suffixes. The sound of the "g" in the words "college," "collegial," and "colleague" is an example. Another complicating factor in English is the retention of historical spellings such as the "gh" in ghost (which is pronounced differently from the "gh" in neighborhood) and the "ph" in geography. Many other examples of spelling patterns that make the sound-symbol relationship so difficult to understand come easily to mind.

> *"Reading is the most complex of human functions." (Shaywitz, 2003)*

Some Learn to Read Easily, Others Don't. Why?

We would be willing to bet that most people do not remember more than the sketchiest details of the process they undertook in learning to read. They may remember the alphabet chart strung across the front of the classroom, their basal reader, the teacher writing a story as they dictated, or matching pictures to words on a worksheet. Nevertheless, they probably have no memory of how and when they finally made sense out of the written symbols to the point where they could read fluently and comprehend what they were reading.

> *We would be willing to bet that most people do not remember more than the sketchiest details of the process they undertook in learning to read.*

What eventually happens to all fluent readers is that the process of decoding becomes automatic. They decode without conscious thought. This ability to carry out an act unconsciously occurs not only in reading, but in many other habits and skills such as driving a car, tying shoelaces, playing the piano, or swinging a golf club. When someone first learns a skill, every aspect is consciously attended to. But over time, and with a great deal of practice, the brain "remembers" how to carry out all the procedures involved in the skill, allowing it to attend consciously to something else. This type of automatic processing is called *unconscious* or *implicit memory*. It comes into play in reading by allowing the reader to concentrate on the meaning of what is being read without having to think about deciphering every word. The downside to this unconscious memory is that knowledge about how this unconscious task is accomplished becomes very difficult to access. As a result, there has been no clear picture of the processes and procedures involved in learning to read. This partially explains the amount of intense debate over which teaching methods work best.

In order to become a fluent reader, certain pre-reading skills need to be mastered, but emergent readers do not all learn these skills in the same way and at the same rate. A small percentage of children learn to read on their own with no formal instruction before they enter kindergarten. Others learn to read fairly quickly once exposed to instruction. However, too many children struggle throughout their school careers, never learning to read well enough to comprehend what they are reading. Why this disparity? The answer to this question is complex. However, to begin to understand reading difficulties, two major factors, one biological and the other environmental or instructional, need to be explored.

> *What eventually happens to all fluent readers is that the process of decoding becomes automatic.*

Some Problems Have a Biological Basis

One possible reason that some children have difficulty learning to read is that these children have a biological or neurological deficit. As neuroscience research has expanded, researchers are acquiring a better understanding of what goes on in the brain when one reads. Using brain-imaging techniques, scientists now have a tentative picture of the brain components involved in reading. A problem with any of these structures has the potential to affect a child's ability to read. Dyslexia, for example, appears to have a biological basis. While specific structures involved in this disorder are often difficult to pinpoint, Sally Shaywitz and her colleagues are beginning to make progress in identifying parts of the brain that play a role in this disorder. This and other research on dyslexia will be addressed later in this book.

Occasionally, adverse pregnancy or labor events can cause severe learning and/or reading problems (Berninger & Richards, 2002). Auditory and/or memory processing difficulties—found in an estimated 20 percent of all children—are additional causes of reading problems (Honig, 2001). Genetic factors have also been implicated in some reading disabilities (Pennington, 1989; Scarborough, 1989). Hearing or visual impairment, verbal memory problems, and attention deficit/hyperactivity disorder (ADHD) are other risk factors.

> *One possible reason that some children have difficulty learning to read is that these children have a biological or neurological deficit.*

Looking at genetic and biological factors, it is easy to see why we might assume that a child's intelligence quotient (IQ) would determine future reading success. This, however, does not appear to be the case. The results of a number of empirical studies on the correlation between IQ

> *The results of a number of empirical studies on the correlation between IQ and reading achievement have shown that IQ is not a strong predictor of reading achievement . . .*

and reading achievement have shown that IQ is not a strong predictor of reading achievement, unless we are looking at children with severe cognitive deficiencies who usually develop very low, if any, proficiency in reading (Stanovich, Cunningham, & Cramer, 1984).

Care needs to be taken when attributing reading problems purely to biological factors. Discovering that a child has a brain system that is not functioning correctly says little about the possibility for remediation. Young children's brains are remarkably plastic or open to change. Biological factors can be altered by the environment, in this case by the reader's experiences, which leads to the second set of factors influencing whether a child becomes a fluent reader—environmental factors.

Other Problems Stem From Environmental Factors

Unfortunately, many children are capable of learning to read but do not because of environmental circumstances. Three major categories of circumstances influence whether children with no biological deficits will reach their reading potential.

Instructional Factors. If the instruction provided by a school is ineffective or inefficient, a child's progress in learning to read will likely be impeded. Without a thorough understanding of the processes involved in reading, it is difficult to design an effective reading curriculum or methods for teaching. There has been little consensus on curriculum or instructional methods, resulting in huge pendulum swings with first one program and then another promising to make all children fluent readers. Debates have raged over which method "works." The recent whole-language versus phonics debate is an example.

Publishers of reading programs have understandably followed the swings, often with little or no understanding of the processes involved in learning to read. Some published materials are poorly constructed and even contain inaccuracies. To add to the problem, programs are often adopted by uninformed committees based on the attractiveness of the illustrations or the number of workbooks and other supplemental materials they provide. Let's face it, educators have not always been the most credible consumers of appropriate curriculum, the authors included!

Why are educators uninformed consumers? One problem is that even when research has provided good information on reading instruction or evidence of the potential effectiveness of a particular program or methodology, the results seldom find their way into the schools. Many teachers assigned to teach reading have had little instruction in the theoretical and biological underpinnings of the reading process. The fact that many teachers are not well prepared to teach reading is a critical issue, as much research supports the importance of the teacher (Allington, 1989; Dykstra, 1967). Alan Farstrup, executive director of the International Reading Association, states, "The expert teacher, professionally trained and experienced in delivering excellent reading instruction, is the most important variable in achieving reading success" (Farstrup, 2000).

Although the selection of reading programs is important, not all reading programs are equally effective in all situations. Teachers' abilities to identify the individual needs of their students and adjust their instruction accordingly often determine whether a particular program will be effective.

When poor instruction occurs consistently, especially in the first year, many students are likely to fall behind. Even if students are exposed to adequate instruction in subsequent years, there is evidence that poor instruction in first grade has long-term effects (Pianta, 1990). Several studies have documented that the poor first-grade reader continues to be a poor reader (Francis, Shaywitz, Stuebing, Shaywitz, & Fletcher, 1996; Torgesen & Burgess, 1998).

Socioeconomic, Ethnic, and Second-Language Factors. Children of all social, ethnic, and economic groups experience reading problems. However, failure to read well is more common among nonwhite children, poor children, and nonnative speakers of English. The reasons are complex. For example, Spanish-speaking students, who make up the largest group of limited-English-proficient (LEP) students in the United States, are particularly at risk. One obvious reason is the language difference itself, as evidenced by the fact that when these students are taught to read in Spanish, many achieve excellent reading capabilities. However, this is not the only explanation. Many children in good bilingual programs still fall behind their English-speaking peers (Slavin & Madden, 1994).

Low socioeconomic status (SES) also appears to play a role in reading achievement, although there is no consensus as to why. One possible explanation is that low-SES children tend to go to inferior schools where there are fewer educational opportunities. Another is that, unlike parents in middle-income homes, many low-SES parents provide fewer opportunities for informal literacy learning, defined as visits to the library, joint book reading, play with print, and independent reading (Baker, Serpell, & Sonnenschein, 1995).

Early Language Development. As we shall see in Chapter 3, there is a close relationship between reading and language. In some children, inability to achieve reading proficiency seems to be attributable to a lack of exposure to language patterns and literacy-based interactions and materials during their early years (National Institute of Child Health and Human Development, 1998). According to author Jane Healy, too many children are being raised in a language-impoverished environment where they are seldom read or talked to and too much time is spent passively viewing television or playing video games (Healy, 1985). This environment develops receptive/listening skills but not the language skills that will be more important when the child begins formal reading instruction.

As with the development of all human abilities, genetic and biological factors cannot be dismissed or minimized in considering the ability to become a competent reader. However, whether a child becomes that reader is also dependent on the environment in which the child is raised. As author Ronald Kotulak so beautifully puts it, the genes are the building blocks of human development, but the environment is the on-the-job foreman (Kotulak, 1996).

> *There is a close relationship between reading and language.*

THE BASICS OF READING

If teachers are asked to list all the skills a child needs in order to read, they might have some difficulty. As mentioned earlier, for nearly all adults, the act of reading has become an unconscious activity, its processes stored in a type of memory called implicit or unconscious memory. In the beginning, every step was a conscious process that had to be learned. Eventually, with a great deal of practice, reading gradually becomes a seamless, automatic activity carried out by the brain without conscious awareness. As with any task that has reached the point of being automatic, the act of reading is difficult to understand (and equally difficult to teach), unless we break it down into its component parts. Many studies have focused on the act of reading, attempting to define each skill in the complex task of becoming a fluent reader who comprehends the meaning of print. Even before children learn to read in the conventional sense, most have acquired information about the purposes and component skills of reading.

> *. . . for nearly all adults, the act of reading has become an unconscious activity, its processes stored in a type of memory called implicit or unconscious memory.*

Emergent Literacy Skills

Some children on entering school and beginning formal reading instruction are much more successful than other children. What makes the difference?

Although—as was mentioned earlier—biological factors are sometimes involved, many times the reason for the differences can be traced to the children's literacy development in the early years before they begin formal schooling.

Emergent literacy skills (sometimes called early childhood readiness skills or pre-reading skills) are terms used by both researchers and educators to describe the skills acquired in early childhood that prepare these children to gain the greatest benefit from formal reading instruction when they enter school. These emergent literacy skills have been shown to have a high correlation with later reading ability (Scarborough, 1989). The National Research Council states that reading is typically acquired relatively predictably by children who have normal or above-average language skills and have had experiences in early childhood that foster motivation and provide exposure to literacy in use (Snow et al., 1998).

We will begin by looking at two emergent literacy skills that appear to be highly predictive factors for reading ability. To the fluent reader, these skills may seem so commonsense as not to be worthy of mention, but they are critical. If ignored, they put at risk the child who is tackling the difficult job of decoding print.

Knowledge About Books

It is easy to forget that young children do not necessarily know what a book is or how it is used. As we read to children, they learn how to hold a book and that it is opened at the beginning. Children also must learn that in English a book is read from left to right and that it is print, not pictures, that is being read. We take this latter skill for granted, but given the vivid and colorful illustrations in children's books, it is easy to see why children might think the pictures are being read (Adams, 1990).

Recognizing the Alphabet

English is an alphabetic language. Thousands of words are derived from a base alphabet of 26 letters. A predictive factor for learning to read is the fast and accurate skill of naming and recognizing these letters. According to Adams, who has done an exhaustive review of the research in this area, this skill is one of the best predictors of first-grade reading ability (Adams, 1990). Although many children are able to recite the alphabet song, letter knowledge goes beyond singing the song. Children must also be able to recognize the letters in many contexts—within words, handwritten or typed,

> A predictive factor for learning to read is the fast and accurate skill of naming and recognizing these letters.

in different fonts, and so on. But accuracy of recognition alone is not enough. The speed at which they can reliably name individual letters appears to be the determining factor. Why are letter recognition and naming such good predictors of later reading success? The names of most letters are closely related to their sounds. As children learn to name the letters, they are beginning to learn their sounds as well. This leads to what Adams feels is the single most important thing children must understand when learning to read: the **alphabetic principle,** which is the understanding that letters have corresponding sounds that make words when combined (Adams, 1990).

Reading Skills

Reading is composed of two main processes: decoding and comprehension. These two processes are independent of one another, but both are necessary for literacy. Decoding involves being able to connect letter strings to the corresponding units of speech that they represent in order to make sense of print. Comprehension involves higher-order cognitive and linguistic reasoning, including intelligence, vocabulary, and syntax, which allow children to gain meaning from what they read. We will begin with a look at the component skills of the decoding process.

> *Reading is composed of two main processes: decoding and comprehension.*

Awareness That Speech Is Composed of Individual Sounds

A discussion of reading requires that we communicate using a common vocabulary. However, the terms used to define the components of the reading process can sometimes be confusing. Consider the following terms: phonological awareness, phonics, phonemic awareness, cipher knowledge, syntax, semantics, lexical knowledge, graphemes, morphemes, onset and rime, and the alphabetic principle. Let's begin with the term that is newest in the lexicon of reading vocabulary and is an essential element of decoding—phonemic awareness.

Although no magic bullet exists for mastering the complex skill of reading, there is a growing consensus that phonemic awareness is a critical piece of the puzzle. Many children appear unable to read well because they lack this skill (Adams, 1990; Clachman, 1991; Torgesen, 1993). Phonemic awareness is a relatively new term for many educators. Exactly what are phonemes and why is phonemic awareness so important? **Phonemes** are the smallest sounds of speech that correspond to the letters of an alphabetic writing system. They are the basic building blocks of spoken words. In English, there are an almost infinite number of possible words, but there are only about 40 to 44 phonemes. For example, the spoken word "cat" is composed of three phonemes, /c/, /a/, and /t/. A new word can be made by deleting a phoneme (delete the /c/ to make the word "at"), replacing a phoneme (replace the /c/ with /b/ to make the word "bat"), or rearranging the phonemes (put the /t/ in the initial position to make the word "tab").

Phonemic awareness is an understanding of the simple fact that a few phonemes can be arranged to make many different words. We want to emphasize that we are talking about spoken language and not to confuse phonemic awareness with awareness of print. How do you know if children have phonemic awareness? They can segment the sounds in words. For example, they can pronounce the first sound they hear in the word "tap," or the last sound in the word "mop."

> *Phonemic awareness is an understanding of the simple fact that a few phonemes can be arranged to make many different words.*

Babies are born with the neural hardware to pronounce all the phonemes in English, as well as the sounds of all other languages. However, the sounds they hear repeatedly strengthen certain neural connections, while the neural connections for the ones they do not hear begin to fade away (Kuhl, Williams, Lacerda, Stevens, & Lindblom, 1992). Research has shown that as early as one month of age, infants distinguish between phonemes such as /ba/ and /p/ (Eimas, Siqueland, Jusczyk, & Vigorito, 1971).

> *Babies are born with the neural hardware to pronounce all the phonemes in English, as well as the sounds of all other languages.*

Before long, babies begin to produce the sounds (phonemes) of their native language, much to the delight of parents who reward their efforts with smiles and repeat the sounds back to the children. In this way, phonemes are encoded deeply in the brain. However, as with many skills and habits embedded in implicit memory, children are not consciously aware of their knowledge. As Marilyn Jager Adams states in her seminal book *Beginning to Read*, "To learn an alphabetic script, we must learn to attend to that which we have learned not to attend to" (Adams, 1990, p. 66).

Phonological Awareness

A term that is often confused with phonemic awareness is **phonological awareness**. This is a broader umbrella term that includes phonemic awareness and the additional skills of recognizing and producing rhymes, breaking words into syllables, distinguishing parts of syllables, and so forth. This latter skill involves identifying onsets and rimes. An **onset** is the initial consonant(s) sound of a syllable and a **rime** is the part of a syllable that contains the vowel and all that follows it in a syllable. For example, in the word "sit," the onset is /s/ and the rime is /it/, and in the word "bag," the onset is /b/ and the rime is

/ag/. Phonological processing can be simple, as in the previous examples, or it can be more complex, such as detecting an accented syllable or determining the roots or prefixes of words.

Note that some authors and researchers do not use the term *phonemic awareness*. Instead, they use the term *phonological awareness* to represent the awareness of phonemes as well as awareness of syllables, onsets and rimes, and so on. Regardless of the terminology, it is important to emphasize that we are talking about the sounds of spoken language, not print. Activities and tasks to teach phonemic and phonological awareness at developmentally appropriate times will be addressed in Chapter 4.

The Alphabetic Principle

Thus far, we have been discussing children's understanding of the sounds of spoken language. Phonemic and phonological awareness are prerequisites for the next stage in learning to read—an understanding of the alphabetic principle. Simply stated, the **alphabetic principle** is the understanding that there is a generally predictable relationship between the sounds of spoken language (**phonemes**) and the letters and spellings that represent those sounds in written language (**graphemes**). To master decoding, children must first make the connections between the sounds in speech and the printed symbols on the page. This insight does not come naturally to most children; it needs to be taught. The methods used to teach children that the sounds are represented by letters are called **phonics**. The term *phonics* often engenders visions of isolated drills, overreliance on worksheets, or rote memorization of phonics rules. Effective phonics instruction is none of these. As we shall see in a future chapter, for many children, systematic instruction in this stage of reading development serves the essential purpose of helping readers figure out as quickly as possible the pronunciation of unknown words, freeing them from relying excessively on pictures or context.

Fluency and Comprehension

We read for a purpose. As important as developing the ability to decode print is, it is a useless skill unless it results in a fluent reader who comprehends what is being read. The final step in reading is to be able to decode so automatically and unconsciously that the conscious processing functions of the brain are totally available for understanding the content of the print.

Fluency and comprehension are separate processes. A person can be a fluent reader without comprehending what is being read. For example, Jane Healy, in her

> *A person can be a fluent reader without comprehending what is being read.*

book *Your Child's Growing Mind*, describes an unusual group of children, called *hyperlexics*, who teach themselves to read as early as 2 years of age. They read obsessively and fluently, but when tested for comprehension, they cannot understand the meaning of a first-grade story. Healy calls reading without comprehension "barking at print" (Healy, 1987).

Reading, Writing, and Literacy

The title of this book indicates that our primary concern is understanding how the brain of a child masters the processes of decoding print and eventually reads with fluency and comprehension. However, learning to read without stumbling, while essential, is not sufficient. Literacy takes a variety of forms from reading a listing in a phone book to researching and writing a dissertation. Regardless of the difference in cognitive requirements of these activities, they all require the reader to move beyond decoding to understanding and often require being able to express that understanding in written form. Literacy is much broader than just being able to decode print. It involves writing, spelling, and other creative and analytical acts. While it is not our primary emphasis, throughout this book we will address some of these broader literacy skills, particularly the development of writing and spelling skills.

> *Literacy takes a variety of forms from reading a listing in a phone book to researching and writing a dissertation.*

REFLECTIVE QUESTIONS

1. Explain why reading in English is more difficult than reading in some other languages.

2. List and discuss at least two biological factors that can cause reading problems.

3. If you are reading this book as part of a study group, assign three people to make short presentations on the three environmental factors that impact reading ability, instructional, socioeconomic, and early language development.

4. Many children come to school without the prerequisite skills for reading. What are these skills and how might educators influence their acquisition?

5. Assume you are making a presentation to parents of kindergarten and/or first-grade students. How would you distinguish the difference between phonemic awareness and phonological awareness? How would explain the alphabetic principle?

What Happens in the Brain When Children Read?

2

BRAIN BASICS

If educators are to make serious progress in solving the reading problems experienced by many children, efforts will need to be based on more than ideological debates on methodologies.

A systematic study of the brain may offer the best hope. Since the 1980s, we have seen a tremendous explosion of research on brain structure and function. We've learned more in the past few years than in all of history. New brain-imaging techniques that show which parts of the brain are active when a person is engaged in various activities have increased tremendously our understanding of how the brain functions. For educators to benefit from this research and begin to apply it in classrooms requires a basic understanding of these structures and their roles. First, we will take a look at the overall structure (macrostructure) of the brain, then we will go a little deeper into the brain and look at the smaller brain structures and systems (microstructure) involved in learning to read a written language.

> *New brain-imaging techniques that show which parts of the brain are active when a person is engaged in various activities have increased tremendously our understanding of how the brain functions.*

Macrostructures

The human brain weighs only about 3 pounds, but its light weight belies its importance. All behavior has its roots in the operations of the brain.

A large fissure running from the back (posterior) of the brain to the front (anterior) divides the top of the brain into two hemispheres, a right and a left. Each hemisphere has its own specialties, but the hemispheres work in concert because they are joined by a huge band of nerve fibers called the **corpus callosum**. These specialties will be further delineated as we begin to look at the processes involved in language and reading.

The outer one-quarter-inch-thick layer covering both hemispheres is called the **cerebral cortex**. (*Cortex* is the Latin word for "bark.") Within the cortex lie the abilities that make us uniquely human—the abilities to take in and process sensory data, communicate using language, be aware of what we are thinking (consciousness), recall the past and plan for the future, be aware of our emotions, create theories, move our body parts, and a myriad of other functions,

> *The human brain weighs only about 3 pounds, but its light weight belies its importance. All behavior has its roots in the operations of the brain.*

including our ability to read. Each hemisphere is divided into four lobes. See Figure 2.1.

Starting at the very back of the brain are the **occipital lobes**, which are primarily responsible for taking in and interpreting visual stimuli. The cortex covering the occipital lobes is often called the *visual cortex*. Above the occipital lobes at the back of the brain are the **parietal lobes**, which receive tactile information (pressure, temperature, pain, etc.) and are responsible for integrating this information with sights and sounds. The **temporal lobes** are located on the sides of the brain above the ears. The cortex covering them is called the *auditory cortex*. The temporal lobes are responsible for taking in and interpreting auditory stimuli. Structures within the temporal lobes also control the production of speech and memory. Right behind the forehead and extending back over the top of the brain are the **frontal lobes**. The cortex covering these lobes is referred to as the *association cortex*.

Two individual parts of the cerebral cortex deserve special attention. (See Figure 2.2.) Toward the back of the frontal lobes is a strip of cells called the **motor cortex**. It stretches across the top of the brain like a headband and controls all motor functions except reflexes. Different sections of this strip govern the movements of specific muscles in the body. Immediately behind the motor cortex lies the *somatosensory cortex*. Just as the motor cortex sends messages out to the various muscles in the body about how and when to move, the somatosensory cortex receives information from the environment about temperature, the position of our limbs, sensations of pain, and pressure. As with the motor cortex, each part of the body is represented by a specific area on the surface of the somatosensory cortex.

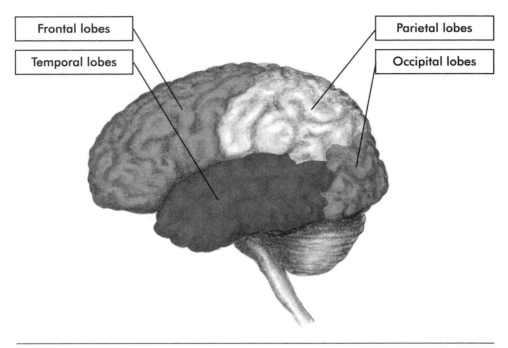

Figure 2.1   The brain with the four lobes labeled.

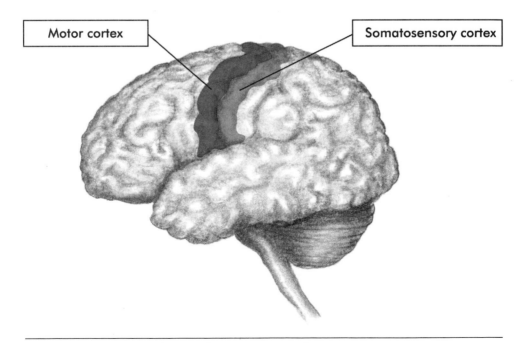

Figure 2.2   The brain showing the motor cortex and somatosensory cortex.

Microstructures

Almost anything a person does, from moving a hand to picking up a glass to reading a book, requires unbelievable coordination among numerous small brain structures. As we begin to look at some of these microstructures of the brain, note that although each micro-structure is addressed separately, none of them works alone. No one area of the brain is devoted to "comprehension" or "semantics." Rather, every task or function involves an interconnected group of structures. Each area within the group makes a specific contribution to the performance of the task. Therefore, trying to determine the exact functions of a specific part of the brain or the neural pathways involved in language or reading is a challenge.

> *Almost anything a person does, from moving a hand to picking up a glass to reading a book, requires unbelievable coordination among numerous small brain structures.*

For years, scientists have worked to understand the brain processes involved in language, but they were limited to studies of the brains of people whose language problems were caused by neurological disease, strokes, or other injuries that often caused some type of *aphasia*. (Aphasia is the partial or complete loss of language abilities following damage to the brain.) During the last two decades of the twentieth century, however, exciting new brain-imaging techniques have allowed scientists to picture the normal brain at work processing language.

Two of the imaging techniques used most frequently by neuroscientists are positron emission tomography (PET) and functional magnetic resonance imaging (fMRI). Simply defined, PET imaging traces the amount of glucose used by the cells of different structures of the brain as a person is engaged in various mental activities. It requires that radioactive glucose be injected into the bloodstream. fMRI, on the other hand, is less invasive as it does not require the injection of any substance. Rather, this imaging technique measures the amount of oxygen being used by the cells. It has the added advantage of showing more precisely where the mental activity is taking place because fMRIs, like regular MRIs, allow scientists to view soft tissue in the body.

> *Two of the imaging techniques used most frequently by neuroscientists are positron emission tomography (PET) and functional magnetic resonance imaging (fMRI).*

Although the way the brain works while normally processing language is not thoroughly understood, most researchers agree that there are several structures and areas central to language. As we have mentioned, reading and writing press into use the structures and pathways used to speak and understand language, so we will begin by looking at these structures.

Brain Structures Involved in Language

Language is a kind of code consisting of a set of spoken symbols that represent the words of the language. Once we break the code, we can understand the language. Language is a very complex code, however, requiring us to manipulate all its forms (words, sentences, and intonation) that refer to objects, actions, and thoughts (Caplan, 1995). What goes on in the brain when we select our words, activate the sounds for each word, select the correct order of words to form a sentence (the syntax), and finally determine the proper intonation to convey the meaning?

> *Language is a kind of code consisting of a set of spoken symbols that represent the words of the language.*

Auditory Cortex. Much language is generated in response to information coming into the brain from the environment, for example, during a conversation with another person. The first stepping-stone on the language pathway is for the brain to recognize that the stimulus being received is sound. The structures that make this preliminary distinction are the *thalamus* and the *auditory cortex*. The thalamus is the receiving point for all incoming sensory data (with the exception of smell), and its job is to act as a sort of relay station, sending messages to the appropriate part of the cortex for further processing. In this case, the sound stimulus is sent to the primary auditory cortex, which is located in the front of the temporal lobe. The thalamus and the auditory cortex appear to work in concert to determine if the incoming stimulus is language or some other type of sound such as environmental noise, music, or random noise. Once the sounds have been identified as language, the next stepping-stone on the pathway is **Wernicke's area**.

Wernicke's area. Named for its discoverer, Austrian neurologist Karl Wernicke, this group of cells is located at the junction of the parietal and temporal lobes in the left hemisphere very near the auditory cortex. (For about nine out of ten right-handed and nearly two-thirds of left-handed people, the major language structures reside in the left hemisphere; Restak, 2001.) The traditional view of Wernicke's area is that it is the semantic processing center and that it plays a significant role in the conscious comprehension of the spoken words by both the listener and the speaker. It appears to contain a sort of lexicon that stores memories of the sounds that make up words. It uses this internal "dictionary" to determine whether the incoming phoneme patterns or words are meaningful.

In this sense, words are not understood until they are processed by Wernicke's area. People who have had damage to this particular area of the brain (called *Wernicke's aphasia*) have no difficulty speaking; however, much of their speech makes no sense. These people also lack the ability to monitor their own speech and do not appear to be aware that they are substituting nonwords for real ones and that to the listener much of what they are saying is meaningless (Carter, 1998). Persons with Wernicke's aphasia also have difficulty comprehending what others are saying to them.

The Arcuate Fasiculus and Broca's Area. Our language pathway is not yet complete. There are two remaining stepping-stones, both controlled by the second major language area of the left hemisphere. The first is the **arcuate fasiculus.** Information leaving Wernicke's area needs to reach the frontal language regions of the brain in order for speech to occur. This feat is accomplished by means of a band of neural fibers called the arcuate fasiculus. Damage to this connecting pathway can result in what is called *conduction aphasia*, where people are not able to repeat what is said to them because the incoming words from Wernicke's area cannot be passed on to the area of the brain responsible for articulation.

The next stepping-stone on the language pathway is called **Broca's area**. This brain region was named for the French neurologist Paul Broca, who first discovered it in the late 1860s. Located in the left hemisphere at the back of the frontal lobe, Broca's area was originally thought to be primarily involved in language production. It has often been referred to as the expressive language center of the brain. Adjoining the section of the motor cortex that controls the jaw, larynx, tongue, and lips, Broca's area appears to convert words into a code to direct the muscle movements involved in speech production. People who have damage to this area (called *Broca's aphasia*) produce a sort of halting, "telegraphic" speech using nouns, verbs, and adjectives while often omitting conjunctions and other parts of speech.

> Recent studies have suggested that while it does control production of speech, Broca's area—probably along with some of the surrounding cortical structures—has a second major language function, that of processing syntax, or assembling words into sensible phrases that are grammatically correct.

Recent studies have suggested that while it does control production of speech, Broca's area—probably along with some of the surrounding cortical structures—has a second major language function, that of processing syntax, or assembling words into sensible phrases that are grammatically correct. This ability to organize the words is essential for meaning. A string of words becomes a sentence only when appropriate grammatical constructions are in place.

Language in the Right Hemisphere. Although the left hemisphere is nearly always dominant for language processing, this does not mean that the right hemisphere plays no role. Studies of persons with right hemispheric damage and of "split-brain" subjects (persons whose hemispheres cannot communicate with one another because the corpus callosum, the band of fibers connecting the two hemispheres, has been surgically severed) have shown that the right hemisphere can read and understand simple sentences. However, the major role that the right hemisphere seems to play is in the affect given to spoken language. A stroke or lesion in the language areas of the right hemisphere does not affect the ability of a person to speak, but his or her speech is devoid of emotional content. Other right hemispheric functions, such as appreciating humor and metaphor, are also often affected by stroke or trauma.

A Caveat. Although the terms *Broca's area* and *Wernicke's area* are commonly used, these language areas are not neat modules with clearly defined borders. A danger exists of overstating the significance of a given cortical area for a particular

> *A danger exists of overstating the significance of a given cortical area for a particular function, as it may be that each area is involved in more than one language function. (Gazzaniga, 1998)*

function, as it may be that each area is involved in more than one language function (Gazzaniga, 1998). The areas of the brain associated with language—its reception, comprehension, processing, and production—are still being studied. As mentioned earlier, it is difficult to map the detailed functions of the language system directly onto the brain's complex anatomical structures. Given these constraints, scientists have, however, produced a tentative architecture of the brain's language pathway that has fairly accurate validity and is useful in our quest to understand what goes on in the brain when we process both spoken and written language (Bear, Conners, & Paradiso, 1996). See Figure 2.3.

Brain Structures Involved in Reading

One of the miracles of the brain is that engaging in a conversation involves all the brain macrostructures and microstructures just described, but learning how to talk does not require an understanding of them or conscious attention to their

> *One of the miracles of the brain is that engaging in a conversation involves all the brain macrostructures and microstructures just described, but learning how to talk does not require an understanding of them or conscious attention to their processes.*

processes. While reading these words, fluent readers are not conscious of the structures that are being activated to allow them to process and comprehend the print. However, for some children these processes are not automatic. It is critical for teachers of these children to understand these underlying processes and how they come to be

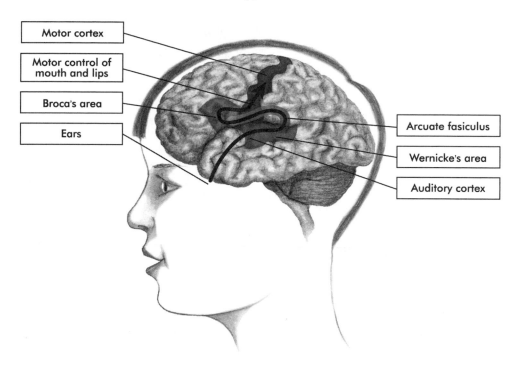

Figure 2.3a   Diagram of the language pathway in the brain.

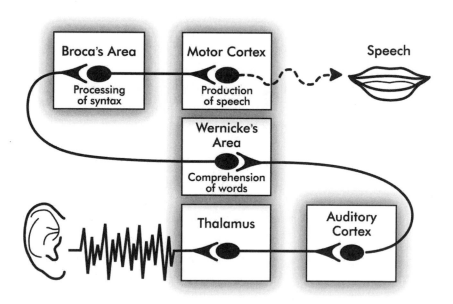

Figure 2.3b   The flow chart of the language pathway.

automatic (or don't). Without this understanding, teachers will not be able to comprehend or use the research on dyslexia and other reading research that is being conducted. Therefore, our next step is to examine the structures (in addition to the ones just discussed) that the brain uses to decode and comprehend print.

The Neural Pathway for Reading

As we have discussed, many of the structures used in reading are the same as those used for spoken language. However, print is a relatively recent invention and requires the brain to co-opt structures that were perhaps designed for other purposes. We will look at two additional areas of the brain that are involved in reading: the *visual cortex* and the *angular gyrus*.

Visual Cortex. The human visual system is one of the most studied and best understood areas of the brain. Although a thorough discussion of this system is beyond the scope of this book, a basic understanding is necessary in order to appreciate its role in the reading process. Visual information is contained in the light that is reflected from objects. As light rays enter the eyes, they are transduced, or changed into electrical impulses, and are sent from the eyes through the optic nerves to the thalamus. The job of the thalamus is to relay this information to the primary visual cortex located in the occipital lobes. It is here in the visual cortex that the brain begins the initial step of reading by recognizing the visual pattern of a word (Gazzaniga, 1998). It does this by calling into use an already existing visual feature extraction system for visual stimuli in general. The brain has adapted this system to allow it to process letter strings, as well as other visual features. Even though the features of the word have been extracted, the string of letters has not been perceived as a word. That job falls partially to another structure, the angular gyrus.

Angular Gyrus. Located at the junction of the occipital, parietal, and temporal lobes, the angular gyrus is perfectly situated to be a bridge between the visual word recognition system and the rest of the language processing system. It is here that the letters of the written words are translated into the sounds or **phonemes** of spoken language. Without this transformation, reading and writing would be impossible. Indeed, damage to the angular gyrus disrupts both reading and writing (Carter, 1998). Sally Shaywitz, in discussing the neurobiology of reading and dyslexia, states that the angular gyrus is pivotal in carrying out cross-modal integration (auditory and visual) and mapping the sights of the print onto the phonemic structures of language (Shaywitz, 2003). In essence,

> *Located at the junction of the occipital, parietal, and temporal lobes, the angular gyrus is perfectly situated to be a bridge between the visual word recognition system and the rest of the language processing system.*

the angular gyrus, in conjunction with Wernicke's area, is the "hub" where all the relevant information about how a word looks, how it sounds, and what it means is tightly bound together and stored (Shaywitz, 2003). From this point forward, processing of the written word follows pretty much the same pathway as spoken language, going from the angular gyrus to Wernicke's area, across the arcuate fasiculus to Broca's area, and, if reading aloud, to the motor cortex.

We can now add to the diagram the additional structures used in the brain for processing written language. (See Figure 2.4.) Remember that the brain is a parallel processor, and the pathway for reading is not as linear as a drawing makes it appear. Also, the specific task affects which structures (in which hemispheres) will be activated. Reading aloud activates different structures from those used in reading silently (Bookheimer, Zeffiro, Blaxton, Gaillard, & Theodore, 1995). Listening to text activates different parts of the brain than does word ordering or syntactic judgments. Which pathways are activated may also depend on how practiced or automatic a task is. However, an understanding of the general functions

> . . . an understanding of the general functions of the structures involved in processing spoken and written language will allow educators to be more informed consumers of reading research and better able to understand how particular neural deficits affect children's ability to read.

of the structures involved in processing spoken and written language will allow educators to be more informed consumers of reading research and better able to understand how particular neural deficits affect children's ability to read.

READING PROBLEMS WITH A BIOLOGICAL BASIS

In Chapter 1, we discussed some of the reasons children fail to learn to read. As was mentioned, some problems stem from genetic or biological factors. Now that we have examined the structures and pathways the brain uses to read, we can look at what happens when one or more of these systems fails to work normally. People whose reading difficulties stem from neurological sources are called

> Dyslexia is a brain disorder that primarily affects a person's ability to read and write. (Bloom et al., 2003)

dyslexic. **Dyslexia** is a brain disorder that primarily affects a person's ability to read and write (Bloom, Beal, & Kupfer, 2003). This disability is separate from intelligence.

Dyslexic persons generally have normal or above-normal intelligence and their higher-order skills are intact. Their problem is not behavioral, psychological,

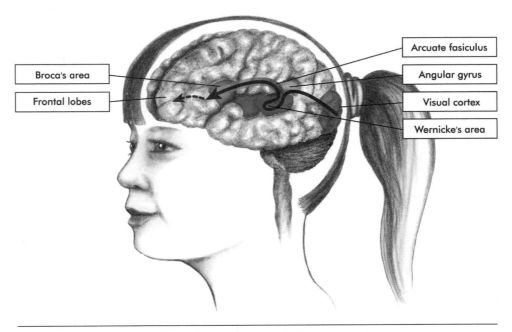

Figure 2.4a   Diagram of the reading pathway in the brain.

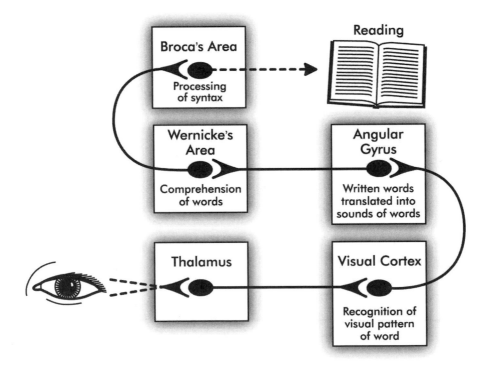

Figure 2.4b   The flow chart of the reading pathway.

motivational, or social. Dyslexia appears to be fairly widespread. While reading experts don't all agree on the prevalence of this disorder, Shaywitz believes that it can be found in as many as 17 percent of school-aged children and as many as 40 percent of the adult population (Shaywitz & Shaywitz, 2001). Dyslexia can be either developmental or acquired as the result of some injury to the brain such as trauma, tumor, or stroke. However, what both developmental dyslexia and acquired dyslexia have in common is a disruption in the neural pathways for reading. People do not outgrow dyslexia. Even though as adults they may become more proficient at reading words, they still have difficulty reading unfamiliar words and are not as fluent or automatic in their reading as a nonimpaired reader (Shaywitz & Shaywitz, 2001).

Visual Processing Problems

Because reading begins with visual input, any problem in the visual system can affect the ability to process print. A growing body of research shows that some poor readers may have subtle sensory deficits in visual processing (Berninger, 2002). These deficits may manifest as poor eye health, poor visual acuity, and/or slower than normal eye movements. Imaging studies of adults with dyslexia conducted at the National Institute of Mental Health (Eden et al., 1996) detected subtle deficits in the visual motion detection area of their brains known as brain region V5/MT. Nonimpaired readers showed robust activity in this area, while persons with dyslexia showed almost no activity. This area of the visual cortex has connections to areas that are active in phonological processing, and it is possible that it plays an important role in the processing of written words.

Although this is a small study and more research needs to be done, Eden et al. believe these findings indicate that dyslexia is a discrete brain disorder and that the source of some reading difficulties may stem from visual deficits rather than problems in the language-related areas. Still other studies are finding that minor differences in how the brain handles the visual processing of images, color, and contrast, as well as fast motion, can impede reading (Eden et al., 1996).

Auditory Processing Problems

Educators are often surprised to learn that in an fMRI or PET scan (which depicts activity levels in the brain) the auditory cortex is active even when a person is reading silently. This occurs because the brain is busy processing all the "sounds" associated with reading, just as it would be if the person were listening to someone speak (Bookheimer et al., 1995). It is not surprising, then, that deficits within the auditory processing areas of the brain are another source of reading problems. These deficits can occur anywhere along the auditory pathway, with the most obvious being a hearing impairment or deafness. Chronic ear infections (chronic otitis media) often lead to intermittent hearing loss in young children and may have a negative effect on language development and, consequently, on reading.

Farther along the auditory pathway, other problems can occur. Recall that, in order to read, children must be able to process the auditory sounds of the language by identifying the sounds (phonemes), linking the phonemes, then associating them to the written words. In English, vowels change relatively slowly, but stop consonants, such as "b" and "p," change more rapidly. Researcher Michael Merzenich and his colleagues at the University of California at San Francisco have discovered that some poor readers do not process these consonant sounds quickly enough (Merzenich et al., 1996). This means that a person with this auditory processing deficit would not be able to clearly distinguish the difference between "bat" and "pat."

Although the original research was conducted with adults, subsequent research has shown that children suffer from the same deficit (Temple et al., 2003). Using a commercially available program (Fast ForWord) that focuses on auditory processing and oral language training, the researchers have been able to train the brains of some dyslexic children to increase the speed and accuracy with which they process rapidly successive and rapidly changing sounds. Brain-imaging scans of these children showed that critical higher-order areas necessary for reading were activated for the first time (Temple et al., 2003). Whether the training results in actual changes in these higher-order areas or if the changes in the basic auditory system are providing information to the higher-order areas is not known at this point (J. Gabrieli, personal communication, April 6, 2003).

Problems in the Language/Reading Pathways

Although many reading difficulties can be attributed to visual or auditory processing deficits, more often the central difficulty appears to be a deficit in the language system. The language pathway of the brain can be conceptualized as a hierarchy of lower- and higher-level skills. At the higher levels are the neural systems that process semantics (the meaning of the language), syntax (organizing words into comprehensible sentences), and discourse (speaking and writing). Underlying these abilities are the lower-level phonological skills dedicated to deciphering the reading code.

> *Although many reading difficulties can be attributed to visual or auditory processing deficits, more often the central difficulty appears to be a deficit in the language system.*

In simple terms, the lower levels handle decoding while the higher levels are dedicated to comprehension. This is a reciprocal process. As a person reads, the brain shifts back and forth between decoding and comprehension. As we have seen, scientists are now able to map the neural structures that process both the higher- and the lower-level skills involved in language and reading. Phonological processing occurs in the back of the left hemisphere (in most people) in the angular gyrus and Wernicke's area. The more skilled readers are, the more they activate this region. Higher-level comprehension skills are handled largely by the frontal regions of the left hemisphere in Broca's area and the frontal lobes. Problems or deficits in either of these areas appear to be central to many reading difficulties.

The Glitch in the System

While educators have long known that poor readers have difficulty "sounding out" unfamiliar words or that they read text without comprehension, there has been little research to help them understand why these problems occur. With the advent of brain-imaging technology, this is changing. Sally and Bennett Shaywitz, pediatricians and neuroscientists at the National Institute of Child Health and Human Development (NICHD)–Yale Center for the Study of Learning and Attention, and their colleagues have conducted some of the most illuminating research.

Using fMRI, a noninvasive imaging technique, these researchers studied 144 children by scanning their brains while they read. The children ranged in age from 7 to 18 years. Seventy were dyslexic readers and 74 were nonimpaired readers. What they discovered is that brain activation patterns differed significantly between the two groups.

In nonimpaired readers, there is activity in both the frontal (Broca's area) and the posterior regions (Wernicke's area and the angular gyrus) in the left hemisphere of the brain. However, in the dyslexic readers, there is a relative underactivation in the posterior areas and a relative overactivation in the frontal regions. As Sally Shaywitz states, "It is as if these struggling readers are using the systems in front of the brain to try to compensate for the disruption in the back of the brain" (Shaywitz, 2003, p. 81). In other words, it appears that the dyslexic readers are using the frontal regions as a sort of "alternative backup" to try to decode, because the areas that would normally serve to interpret the written code are not working as they should. This pattern seems to be universal in dyslexics, no matter which language they speak or what their age. An earlier

> *"It is as if these struggling readers are using the systems in front of the brain to try to compensate for the disruption in the back of the brain." (Shaywitz, 2003, p. 81)*

study conducted by the same team of researchers showed that this failure to activate the phonological processing area of the brain continues into adulthood (Shaywitz & Shaywitz, 2001).

This research shows that there is a physiological basis, or "glitch" in the system, for some reading difficulties. As Sally Shaywitz states, "Most likely as the result of a genetically programmed error, the neural system necessary for phonologic analysis is somehow miswired, and a child is left with a phonologic impairment that interferes with spoken and written language" (Shaywitz, 2003, p. 68).

The most recent research led by Bennett and Sally Shaywitz and their colleagues compared the brain scans of 43 young adults who were impaired (dyslexic) readers with 27 *nonimpaired* readers. These two groups had been followed since elementary school and were from similar socioeconomic backgrounds and had comparable reading skills when they began school. What the researchers discovered was surprising: there appeared to be two distinct types of brain problems in the dyslexic readers. One is predominantly genetic, as reported in the earlier study. These students, as we have seen, appear to have a glitch in their neural circuitry and enlist other parts of their brains to compensate. They can read and comprehend, but they read slowly.

The findings from the second group are even more interesting. The researchers have determined that these readers have what they call "a more environmentally influenced" type of dyslexia. Their brains' systems for processing sounds and language were intact, but the brain scans of these readers showed that rather than using the usual language structures in the left hemisphere to process print, they created an alternate neural pathway, reading mostly with regions in the right hemisphere—areas not as well suited for reading. The portion of the right frontal lobe, which was activated in these readers, is an area that is primarily devoted to memory. These readers appeared to rely on memory to read. This rote-based type of learning can get the student to a certain point, but eventually there is too much to memorize and the system fails. As Sally Shaywitz states,

> *Researchers, using brain imaging, may be able to validate effective strategies for helping struggling readers as they observe changes that take place in the neural systems for reading as the result of specific reading interventions.*

[These] persistently poor readers have a rudimentary system in place, but it's not connected well. They weren't able to develop and connect it right because they haven't had that early stimulation. If you can provide these children early on with effective reading instruction, these children can really learn to read. (Shaywitz et al., 2002)

These exciting new findings have major implications for those who study and teach reading. Researchers, using brain imaging, may be able to validate effective strategies for helping struggling readers as they observe changes that take place in the neural systems for reading as the result of specific reading interventions. Several of these interventions will be discussed in later chapters.

Attention and Memory Systems Involved in Reading

Thus far, we have been examining the physiological structures that the brain has adapted to allow us to read. Attention and memory systems are a bit more difficult to localize in the brain than are the sensory processes. However, an understanding of how the brain's memory systems function is essential to understanding the reading process, since some reading disabilities stem from problems in these areas.

As we have seen, phonemic awareness and phonological awareness are necessary components of reading, but they are not sufficient. In addition, the beginning reader must be able to pay attention to what is being read and needs to have a good memory. What does it mean to pay attention or to have a good memory?

> ... an understanding of how the brain's memory systems function is essential to understanding the reading process, since some reading disabilities stem from problems in these areas.

Actually, it can mean many things. First, let's look at a model that is commonly used to differentiate among the three major memory systems of the brain.

Sensory Memory

Figure 2.5 depicts how the brain takes in or discards incoming information, manipulates it, and stores it. The first box in the diagram is labeled Sensory Memory and depicts the initial stage of information processing, taking in sensory data, and determining what to keep and what to drop. Sensory memory can be thought of as the brain's attention system. Because much of the sensory stimuli impinging on the body—the feeling of

> Sensory memory can be thought of as the brain's attention system.

clothing against the body, for example—is not relevant at any given moment, much of the incoming information, perhaps as much as 99 percent, is immediately discarded. This system is obviously critical to reading. Being able to focus on the letters and words rather than on random stimuli is an initial step in becoming a reader.

Many factors influence a child's ability to focus attention. Inattention to a task can be the result of hunger, fatigue, and other physical factors; the

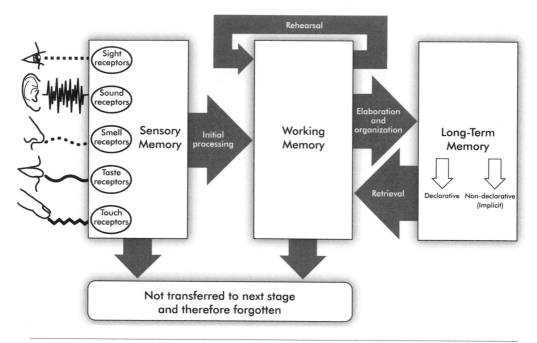

Figure 2.5   Diagram of information processing model.

emotional state of the child; environmental noise and/or temperature; or an inappropriate level of difficulty of the material. Given the right conditions, however, most children have little or no difficulty paying attention to relevant stimuli, but some do. Possibly the most well known, but still poorly understood, biological condition to impact attention is attention deficit/hyperactivity disorder (ADHD).

ADHD is a label given to persons with a neurobiological disorder that interferes with their capacity to attend to tasks and regulate their behavior. Although ADHD and reading disability are distinct disorders, there is good evidence that they often occur together. According to researcher Sally Shaywitz, reading disability is relatively common in children with attention problems. Shaywitz estimates that this occurs in 31 percent of first-grade children, becoming even more frequent as the child grows older. She estimates that over 50 percent of ninth-grade students diagnosed with ADHD have a reading disability (Shaywitz, Fletcher, & Shaywitz, 1994). This disorder is contained to some degree by medication and/or behavioral therapy.

> *ADHD is a label given to persons with a neurobiological disorder that interferes with their capacity to attend to tasks and regulate their behavior.*

Working Memory

The filtering of stimuli that occurs in sensory memory happens so quickly that it is an unconscious process. The brain is continuously taking in sensory stimuli, assembling and sorting the data, and directing only some of it to conscious attention. Although conscious processing represents only a small part of information processing, without it readers would not be able to retain the first part of a sentence as they are reading to its end. This short-term, conscious processing is called **working memory**. Working memory allows the brain to hold on to information for a short time, approximately 18 seconds. However, the brain can retain the information longer by rehearsing it. Researcher William Baddeley coined the term "articulatory loop" to describe this type of rehearsal (Baddeley, 1986).

> *Working memory allows the brain to hold on to information for a short time, approximately 18 seconds.*

Think about being given several directions at a time or trying to remember a phone number long enough to dial it. Most people probably mentally repeated the directions or the number over and over using their own articulatory loop. This verbal rehearsal or subvocalization appears to be essential for comprehension of what is being read. According to research, skilled readers cannot remember—or comprehend—a complex sentence when they are prevented from subvocalizing its wording (Baddeley, 1979). While children can be observed repeating songs and phrases, this is generally not done with a conscious understanding of the need to rehearse to remember information. This understanding of the need to rehearse information to remember it often does not occur spontaneously until around age 7 or 8. However, children can be taught to do this earlier (Kail, 1984). Younger—and poorer—readers often do not engage in this type of rehearsal. This is especially true for children in homes where parents do not understand the necessity of rehearsal strategies.

It is easy to see how the age of a child or a dysfunctional verbal memory negatively affects reading ability. However, the problem may not necessarily be in the articulatory loop. Other aspects of working memory may be completely normal but still work against the reading process. (Remember that even the brain that works normally was not designed for reading.) In order to understand these, we need to become familiar with several other characteristics of a normal working memory that affect the ability to decode and comprehend print.

> *It is easy to see how the age of a child or a dysfunctional verbal memory negatively affects reading ability.*

The Cocktail Party Effect. In a normal environment, paying attention is generally not difficult. However, when the auditory stimuli increase, such as at a cocktail party, the brain has a problem; it can only pay conscious attention to one train of thought at a time. People can *do* two things at the same time if one is automatic. This phenomenon is familiar. Who hasn't arrived at a familiar location without being aware of driving there? The procedure of driving was so automatic that you were able to think through a problem or plan a meal at the same time you were driving.

Think about children who are still in the process of sounding out unfamiliar words as they are reading. In all likelihood, their train of thought—comprehension—is lost when they stop to decode. This would also be true of an adult who is learning to read a second language. It is not that the child or adult has a dysfunctional working memory; it is a normal phenomenon of a brain that is focusing on decoding rather than on comprehension. Educators need to be aware of this processing limitation when working

> *People can do two things at the same time if one is automatic.*

with a beginning reader. After the word(s) has been deciphered, it is generally wise to have the child re-read the sentence, checking to make certain that its meaning is understood. Otherwise, children may come to view reading as a sort of "performing art," not realizing that we read for a purpose.

The Capacity of Working Memory. The ability to retain information in working memory is essential for reading. Readers must be able to remember what they have previously read in order to make sense of what they are presently reading. Therefore, it is important to be aware that memory capacity is developmental and that the age of the children determines how much information they can hold on to at a time.

Researcher Pascual-Leone theorizes that the number of items that can be held in working memory varies with age (Pascual-Leone, 1970). According to Pascual-Leone, in a test requiring a subject to recall strings of digits, the typical 5-year-old can recall two digits. The number of digits children can recall accurately increases by 1 every 2 years until a mental age of 15, when the adult capacity of 7 is reached. However, emergent readers are not recalling digits but engaging in the very complex task of learning to read. The capacity of working memory is relative to the requirements of the reading task. These include

the amount of effort children are having to invest

the speed with which the individual words are decoded

whether children are engaging in verbal rehearsal

the length and complexity of the sentences

What this adds to our efforts to understand reading is that the greater effort readers must invest in the individual words, the less processing "space" they will have to recall the preceding words or phrases when it is time to put them all together. The child's brain could be thought of as being on cognitive overload. One research study found that poorer third-grade readers could not remember as many as three words back in a clause (Goldman, Hogaboam, Bell, & Perfetti, 1980).

Chunking as a Way of Increasing the Capacity of Working Memory. Adults have the ability to hold on to seven bits of information. However, it is easy to think of an example of a string of digits longer than seven that can be recalled without difficulty. How does this happen? The answer is in the definition of a bit. When a certain configuration of numbers or letters is processed many times, the brain eventually stores that particular configuration as a single bit of information.

Let's say, for example, that a beginning reader is introduced to an unfamiliar word such as "cap" and is able to read it by pronouncing each letter sound or phoneme. This act requires using three bits of working memory. However, with repeated exposure to the word "cap," it is recognized as a word, not three separate letters, and the reader no longer has to decode it. It has become automatic and is now stored in working memory as one bit or chunk of information.

> *Our ability to chunk information into larger and larger bits is one of the marvelous qualities of our brains that allows us to read fluently and eventually comprehend what we are reading.*

Michael Pressley (2001) puts it very well in his book *Reading Instruction That Works: The Case for Balanced Teaching:*

> In fact, decoding and comprehension compete for the available short-term capacity. When a reader slowly analyzes a word into component sounds and blends them, a great deal of capacity is consumed, with relatively little left over for comprehension of the word, let alone understanding the overall meaning of the sentence containing the words and the paragraph containing the sentence. In contrast, automatic word recognition consumes very little capacity, and thus frees short-term capacity for the task of comprehending the word and integrating the meaning of the word with the overall meaning of the sentence, paragraph, and text. Consistent with this analysis, uncertain decoders comprehend less than do more rapid, certain decoders. (p. 67)

Our ability to chunk information into larger and larger bits is one of the marvelous qualities of our brains that allows us to read fluently and eventually comprehend what we are reading. When we see how the brain links separate bits of information into larger wholes, we see why repeated exposure to a common vocabulary is essential.

Long-Term Memory

Now that we have looked at how the brain encodes incoming information and manipulates it, we are ready to look at the third part of our model, long-term memory. **Long-term memory** explains how the brain stores that information. There are actually two types of long-term memory: declarative and nondeclarative. Declarative memory is just what its name says, recalled information that can be declared, such as names, events, concepts, and other types of learned data. To bring these data to mind requires conscious thought. Nondeclarative memory, on the other hand, consists of habits and skills that have been practiced to the point that they can be performed unconsciously. For this reason, declarative memory is often called *conscious* or *explicit memory* and nondeclarative labeled *unconscious, procedural, automatic,* or *implicit memory.*

To read fluently with comprehension requires both declarative and nondeclarative memory skills. At this point, we are more interested in nondeclarative memory as it relates to reading. Our conscious working memory, as we have seen, is limited in the amount of information it can handle. One way to reduce this overload is to get certain procedures or skills to the automatic level. In the case of reading, decoding is what we want to become an automatic or unconscious activity. As has been pointed out, unless this occurs, most or all the space in working memory is used for deciphering the print and little or none is left for the higher-level skills involved in comprehending what is being read. Reading the words in this sentence relies on automatic processing so that the reader can focus on the meaning. However, if this sentence contained an unfamiliar word or one in another language, automatic processing would be disrupted while the reader decoded the word. How do fluent readers reach the point of decoding automaticity? What is necessary to assist the beginning reader in reaching this point?

> *Obtaining automaticity in any skill is not as much a matter of the person's innate ability or intellectual prowess as it is of the amount and type of practice in the skill.*

Obtaining automaticity in any skill is not as much a matter of the person's innate ability or intellectual prowess as it is of the amount and type of practice in the skill. While long, tapered legs might be an asset to becoming an expert gymnast, they would be of little value unless the person practiced long and hard under expert guidance. The same is true of becoming an expert reader. No matter what our IQ, we do not have brains that can remember most words after seeing them once. For readers to obtain automatic word recognition, a great deal of the right kind of practice under expert guidance is also necessary.

First, the grapheme-phoneme (letter-sound) relationships need to be matched and experienced so frequently that they begin to be seen automatically as units. As readers put more and more of these units together into words, the same rehearsal with the words is necessary. (Second-language learners often do the opposite of the procedure. They take the pieces they understand and put them into the language structure.) This is accomplished by frequent retrieval of these words in normal reading activities. Gaining automaticity in reading is not an easy process, but when teachers understand the process and provide beginning readers with many opportunities for rehearsal, it happens with nearly all children.

Understanding the systems in the brain that are involved in learning to read is a necessary, but not sufficient, component in our quest to build a reading brain. We now need to look at how an understanding of brain processes can assist us in determining the best methods to use as we guide children on their journey to becoming readers. In the next chapter, we will look at how the foundations for reading are set in the years from birth to age 3.

REFLECTIVE QUESTIONS

1. Assume a colleague has asked you how an understanding of the brain will help her teach reading. How would you respond?

2. Explain the statement, "Reading is an unnatural act for the brain."

3. Discuss the role the right hemisphere normally plays in language.

4. If you are reading this book as part of a study group, ask two people to diagram and explain the differences between the language pathway and the reading pathway.

5. Make an outline for a short faculty presentation about Sally Shaywitz's research and her findings about the "glitch in the system" that causes some children difficulty in learning to read.

Building a Foundation for Reading

3

Birth to Age 3

In a sense, learning to read begins at birth. We don't mean that as soon as a child is born parents should run out and buy a book on how to teach a baby to read. However, one basic element underlies reading: language skills. Since we now know that learning to read depends on well-developed language structures, as well as on the type of life experiences the child has, the process actually does begin at birth.

Not too many years ago, the conventional wisdom was that babies are cute creatures who are not capable of a great deal of learning in the very early years. Recent research has proved the conventional wisdom to be wrong (Gopnik, Meltzoff, & Kuhl, 2000). In the first few years of life, the brain begins to wire itself at a furious pace. Trillions of connections (synapses) are made between the 100 billion neurons the infant has at birth. The experiences of the infant help define which connections are made. This is especially true for the language centers in the cortex. For example, at birth the human brain has the language capacity to pronounce the sounds of over 6,000 languages, including the umlaut "o" in German, the 10 "t" sounds of Hindi, and the trilled "r" of Spanish. Babies are born primed to be multilingual. However, the sounds children hear repeatedly strengthen particular connections in the brain, while the connections for the sounds that are not reinforced eventually fade away (Kuhl, 1992).

> In a sense, learning to read begins at birth.

How does the infant, whose name reflects an inability to speak (*in fantis* means "not speaking"), come to be a proficient speaker? Interestingly, infants begin to practice their native language long before they speak it. They are somehow computing the frequency of the sounds they hear and becoming attuned to these sounds. This amazing ability can most likely be attributed to the brain's neural plasticity. The brain is the only organ in the body that remains plastic throughout life and sculpts itself through its experiences. This marvelous capacity allows the brain to adapt and change its neural patterns in response to its environment. Neuroscientists are fond of saying, "Neurons that fire together, wire together." The synapses that are reinforced are more likely to remain, while those that are not are likely to atrophy.

> *Neuroscientists are fond of saying, "Neurons that fire together, wire together."*

In looking at the development of language, we often focus on the period beginning with the child's first recognizable words at around 1 year of life. However, every day of that preceding year, a variety of language-related mechanisms have been working to prepare the child for speech. In fact, the journey toward language begins *before* birth. Studies have shown that a baby is born recognizing its mother's voice and showing a preference for her voice over others (Locke, 1994).

In the final trimester of pregnancy, the fetus is able to hear its mother's voice within the womb more audibly than the voices of other people, so it is not surprising that the brain becomes attuned to it. It is possible that this prenatal exposure also engenders a preference for the mother's language as well as her voice. Studies by Jacques Mehler and his colleagues at the Laboratoire de Sciences Cognitives et Psycholinguistique found that, as early as 4 days of age, babies born of French-speaking women prefer the sound of French to Russian (Mehler & Christophe, 1994).

Another language-related mechanism is occurring as the infant quickly develops sensitivity to **prosody**, the emotional qualities of speech, such as intonation and rhythm. All people capture meaning from conversations by tracing the rhythm and intonations of spoken language. In fact, these prosodic cues are probably more important to meaning than the actual words. The phrase, "That's great." can be either positive or negative. We determine the meaning by reading facial cues and the intonation of the speaker. Infants develop the ability to recognize these cues as young as 3 months (Jusczyk, 1999).

The language and accompanying emotional emphasis used by parents and caregivers as they talk to infants is often called *Motherese* or *Parentese.* This language, with its elongated vowels, repetitions, and overpronounced syllables, appears to be just what the baby needs to develop its language skills. It models the prosody and sound structure—the phonology, syntax, and lexicon—of the mother tongue. Parentese has also been found to be more grammatically correct (99 and 44/100 percent pure, according to one estimate) than normal speech (Pinker, 1997). The parent is, in a sense, telling the baby how language is structured and to what uses it can be put. It is interesting that Parentese is apparently innate, appearing in every culture and used

> *The language and accompanying emotional emphasis used by parents and caregivers as they talk to infants is often called Motherese or Parentese.*

automatically by anyone who speaks to a baby (Eliot, 1999). In *The Scientist in the Crib*, Gopnik et al. (2000) write, "One thing that science tells us is that nature has designed us to teach babies, as much as it has designed babies to learn."

The springboard for the development of language in infants is probably the social interaction between parent and child. When parents talk and coo to their babies, their speech, as well as their faces, is filled with expression. This encourages and sustains attachment and bonding that is obviously pleasurable for the infant. The baby, in turn, begins to smile, coo, and mimic the parent. Researchers have found that babies as

> *The springboard for the development of language in infants is probably the social interaction between parent and child.*

young as 42 minutes old will copy adults who stick out their tongues (Meltzoff & Moore, 1977). Language in infants appears to be a medium for social and emotional interaction between the babies and those who are important in their environment.

So, how do parents start their infants off on the right track to reading? Not with any formal program, but by following their natural inclination to talk to their infants, smile at them, and express their positive affection. Parental intuition has been scientifically reinforced. The young child's mastery of language, as we shall see, would never proceed normally without the steady dialogic support from parents and other involved adults and siblings.

THE BEGINNINGS OF LANGUAGE

Around 2 to 3 months, the areas of the motor cortex that control the larynx and vocal cords have matured sufficiently to allow babies to begin to vocalize in what we call babbling. In babbling, the babies appear to be experimenting with various ways of making sounds. Even when there are no listeners, they babble to themselves. (Deaf babies also go through a brief stage of babbling, although they give it up after a few months. These babies do, however, begin "babbling" with their fingers around 6 or 7 months of age if they're exposed to sign language; Eliot, 1999.) While they make many different sounds, babies seem to show a preference for the sounds they have heard repeatedly. Peter Jusczyk, a psychologist at the State University of New York, and his colleagues found that 8½-month-olds who heard a simple recorded story several consecutive times listened much longer to words such as "ant" and "jungle" that had been repeatedly mentioned in the story (Jusczyk, 1999).

The repetition of particular sounds begins to strengthen connections for these sounds in the brain. In the book *The Scientist in the Crib*, Patricia Kuhl reports on her findings that babies under the age of 10 months—who have normal hearing—babble in the phonemes of their own language (Gopnik et al., 2000). The baby is beginning to develop a preference for some sounds over others. In a series of experiments, Paul Luce of the State University of New York at Buffalo found that 9-month-old babies listened longer to words containing sound segments that occur frequently in speech than they did to those containing segments that they rarely heard (Luce, 2002). This preference reflects changes that are taking place in the neural connections in the brain. For example, a 6-month-old Japanese infant can still detect the English "l" and "r" sounds. But if exposed only to Japanese in the next 6 months, this baby will lose the ability to hear the difference, and the two phonemes will sound the same. Certain connections have been pruned to adapt the child's brain to the language it hears repeatedly (Deacon, 1997).

> "Babies don't say 'mama' and 'papa' as their first words. They're the first sounds we recognize, and the baby gets a real big reaction. . . .The baby has said 47 other sounds and nobody clapped!" (Leach, 1995)

Repetition and reinforcement appear to play a critical role in the determination of which connections are made and which are pruned. As developmental psychologist Penelope Leach puts it, "Babies don't say 'mama' and 'papa' as their first words. They're the first sounds we recognize, and the baby gets a real big reaction. . . .The baby has said 47 other sounds and nobody clapped!" (Leach, 1995).

Baby Signs

Infants comprehend words and phrases long before they are able to say much of anything. In the second 6 months, even though their first words are still months off, they are beginning to communicate. Linda Acredelo, a professor of psychology at the University of California at Davis, noticed that her own daughter, Katie, had devised her own "baby sign" for the word "flower" by crinkling her nose as if smelling its fragrance. It occurred to Acredelo that, even though Katie could not speak, she was trying to become a partner in conversation. She taught her daughter several other signs and was fascinated with the results. Her daughter could now communicate her understanding of words and concepts through signing.

This led Acredelo and co-researcher Susan Goodwyn of California State University at Stanislaus to study 140 babies starting at 11 months and continuing until the children turned 4. One-third of the families were encouraged to use baby signs, whereas the other two-thirds were not. Acredelo and Goodwyn collected and analyzed nearly 1,000 videotapes of the toddlers in action. The results confirmed what they had hypothesized: the baby sign babies scored higher on an intelligence test, understood more words, had larger vocabularies, and engaged in more sophisticated play. Parents were enthusiastic about the increased communication, decreased frustration, and enriched parent-infant bond (Acredelo & Goodwyn, 1996).

THE LANGUAGE EXPLOSION: 1 TO 2 YEARS

Around 1 year of age, children begin to speak their first words. Although they are beginning to produce speech, they do not yet appear to understand the linguistic rules and they say few words that they have not heard before. They are essentially parroting what others say. This, however, is a critical period in the development of the child's language skills, especially in building vocabulary. From 1 year on, children develop language skills rapidly. At about 18 months, vocabulary explodes with children adding a new word

> At about 18 months, vocabulary explodes with children adding a new word to their vocabulary at the astounding rate of one word every 2 hours or so. (Koralek & Collins, 1997)

to their vocabulary at the astounding rate of one word every 2 hours or so (Koralek & Collins, 1997). Their receptive vocabulary—the words they understand—grows even more rapidly (Eliot, 1999).

While there may be a few months' difference between children, most normal children enter this rapid period of vocabulary growth some time during their second year. It is not surprising that this explosion of vocabulary occurs at the same time there is a spurt in brain development. This period of rapidly expanding language development coincides with the time when synapse formation and metabolic activity are at their highest in the cortex (Eliot, 1999).

Language Development Between 2 and 3 Years

By age 2, nearly all children have between 100 and 200 words in their vocabulary and have begun to combine words to form simple phrases. These phrases are usually word sequences they hear frequently in the speech of others, but spoken in what is called "telegraphic speech"—short phrases containing basic information such as "All gone." or "Daddy play ball." Children's neural pathways for language develop rapidly, and between 24 and 30 months, their sentences become longer and more complete. The child's brain is not only going through a language explosion but through a grammar explosion as well. Children are now beginning to analyze the longer patterns of words that they hear and are experimenting with some rules. For example, they will figure out that you add an "s" for plurals and "ed" for past tense.

Children's brains seem to be hungry for patterns, and while it may appear that children acquire these new skills on their own, studies show that they are the result of considerable, though playful and informal, adult guidance (Anbar, 1986; Durkin, 1996). Now, more than ever, is the prime time to talk with children and read to children. Since children at this age spend little time with peers, adult-child interactions become the critical pathway for the development of the child's brain for language and eventually for reading.

> *Children's brains seem to be hungry for patterns. . . .*

Betty Hart, a professor at the University of Kansas, and Todd Risley, a professor at the University of Alaska at Anchorage, were discouraged with the poor long-term results of a program to teach preschool 3- and 4-year-olds new vocabulary. They decided to study younger children. Hart and Risley spent 2½ years observing 42 families for an hour each month. They wanted to see what typically goes on in the homes with 1- and 2-year-old children who are just learning to talk. They discovered that the children turned out to be like their parents. Approximately 86 percent to 98 percent of the words recorded in each child's vocabulary consisted of words also recorded in their parents' vocabularies. More surprising was the size of the children's vocabularies. The range of words recorded went from 168 for children whose parents were on welfare to 1,116 for children of professional parents. Perhaps not as surprising, a follow-up study showed that the rate of vocabulary growth at age 3 was strongly associated with later performance in school (Hart & Risley, 2003).

The way children learn language, any language, is very predictable, and this shows how deeply rooted language is in our biological makeup. As we have emphasized repeatedly, children are born with a brain programmed for language learning. As neuroscientist Lisa Eliot states in her book *What's Going On in There?* "Children don't really need to be taught language; just talk to them, and you will see their linguistic brain grow and blossom" (Eliot, 1999). This is why it is so important for parents and caregivers to understand the role environment plays.

Parental and Family Influences on Emergent Literacy

Adults who live and interact regularly with children have a profound influence not only on the size of their vocabulary, but also on the quality and quantity of their literacy experiences. While it might appear that there is not much parents can do with a child from birth to age 3 that will influence later reading ability, quite the contrary is true. Parental beliefs and attitudes about reading and literacy, as well as their behaviors, have a large effect on the emerging literacy of the young child (Snow, Burns, & Griffin,

> *Adults who live and interact regularly with children have a profound influence not only on the size of their vocabulary, but also on the quality and quantity of their literacy experiences.*

1998). How important parents believe literacy and reading to be, whether they see reading as a source of entertainment, how aware they are of the functions of reading and writing for gathering information and problem solving, and their expectations for their children's literacy, have all been shown to have a lasting effect on the child's attitude about learning to read (Snow et al., 1998).

Programs That Teach Parents to Teach Children

Many parents are not aware of the role they play in improving their children's outcomes in language and literacy development. Parent-oriented early-intervention programs address this problem by teaching parents and caregivers appropriate strategies to enhance children's language development. Generally, these programs include scheduled home visits by a parent educator. Parents as Teachers (PAT) is one very

> *Many parents are not aware of the role they play in improving their children's outcomes in language and literacy development.*

successful program in which home visits begin in the third trimester of pregnancy and continue until the child is 3. A follow-up study is conducted when the child is in first grade. Children whose parents participated in PAT scored significantly better on standardized tests of reading ability than a comparison group. In addition, the PAT parents were much more involved in their children's school experience than parents in the comparison group.

A synthesis of the research on family literacy programs states "documented research consistently supports the finding that participants in family literacy programs are benefited by increased positive literacy interactions in the home between parent and child as a correlate of their participation" (Tracey, 1994). Many homes have computers, and virtually all homes have television. Both videotapes and television programs can provide a wealth of information to parents regarding literacy development and activities they can do with their children.

Elements of a Literacy-Nurturing Environment

If we could become silent observers in a home during the first 3 years of a child's life, what would we see that would assure us that this child was being provided the best start possible on the road to reading? Research has given us a better understanding of how language develops in the brain and how language provides the foundation for reading. Based on this information, we are now able to identify the environment, activities, and behaviors that enable children to develop their language—and eventually reading—capacity to the fullest.

> *We are now able to identify the environment, activities, and behaviors that enable children to develop their language—and eventually reading—capacity to the fullest.*

Talk, Talk, Talk

Talkative mothers have been vindicated! Providing a rich language culture is just what the developing language pathways in the brain need. Janellen Huttenlocher, a psychologist at the University of Chicago, and her colleagues report on a study they conducted that found that children of the most talkative mothers had 33 more words in their vocabulary at 16 months than did the children of mothers who were the least talkative. At 20 months, the difference was 131 words, and at 24 months, 295.

> *Talkative mothers have been vindicated!*

She states that the differences probably reflect the number of opportunities children had to hear a word and then try it on their own (Huttenlocher, Haight, Bryk, Seltzer, & Lyons, 1991).

Not only does talking to the young child develop vocabulary, it develops background knowledge about a variety of topics. Pointing to and naming objects while shopping at the grocery store, talking about the neighborhood scene while on a walk with the child, naming the foods while preparing a meal, and talking about mundane daily activities while engaged in them, all contribute to the child's background knowledge. Using language formats, such as predictable routine language repetitions at meals and bath times or conversations about other family activities, help children understand that language has order and involves interactions. As children begin to talk, parents should use complete sentences as a way of beginning to informally teach them the syntax and the structure of language. Concerning syntax, it is important to note that there is a critical period for learning the structure of language. Nearly all children can learn to use nouns and verbs correctly, but the critical period for learning grammar (the correct use of articles, conjunctions, and prepositions) appears to wane around age 3. Helen Neville, a cognitive neuroscientist at the University of Oregon, notes that if language learning is left until too late, these systems for grammar will not develop normally (Neville, 1995).

> *Nearly all children can learn to use nouns and verbs correctly, but the critical period for learning grammar (the correct use of articles, conjunctions, and prepositions) appears to wane around age 3.*

The Single Most Important Intervention

According to a 1985 study by the National Commission on Reading, reading aloud to children is the single most important intervention for developing their literacy skills. The research is clear—children who are read to from an early age are more successful at learning to read. Linguist Noam Chomsky notes that one of the most important activities for building the knowledge and skills eventually required for reading is reading aloud to children (Chomsky, 1972). Many studies confirm the positive long-term effects of story reading on children's vocabulary and story comprehension (Dickinson & Smith, 1994; Teale, 1984). There are several reasons reading to children produces such distinct benefits. First, it increases their vocabulary and helps them become familiar with language patterns. Repetition increases the strength of neural connections. Reading the same book to children repeatedly—which they love—serves to reinforce familiar words.

> *According to a 1985 study by the National Commission on Reading, reading aloud to children is the single most important intervention for developing their literacy skills.*

Children often become so familiar with the vocabulary of a favorite story they can "read" it with an adult or pretend to read it to a sibling or to one of their dolls or stuffed animals.

A second benefit of reading to children is that the child acquires familiarity with the reading process. The pre-reading child has much to learn about print—how the book is turned when it is "right side up"; that the print is read, not the pictures; that you start at the beginning of the page and after finishing that page, turn to the next; and so on. Children learn about reading by observing others read to them. The benefit of reading to a child is further enhanced when the reader involves the child by asking him or her to point to or name pictures of persons or objects, points out objects in the story that are present in the child's own environment, encourages the child to retell the story, or otherwise involves the child in some type of discussion.

When adults set aside a special time to read to children each day and read with obvious enjoyment and enthusiasm, they are identifying reading as a pleasurable activity and increasing the probability that the children will view it in the same way. Reading a variety of books, including those that explore common, everyday objects and events, is another excellent way to build the child's background knowledge.

> *Children learn about reading by observing others read to them.*

The "Nursery Rhyme Effect"

> Pat-a-cake, pat-a-cake, baker's man.
> Bake me a cake as fast as you can.
> Roll it and pat it and mark it with a "B,"
> And pop it in the oven for baby and me.

Why have we included a nursery rhyme in a book on reading? When two sounds are similar, they excite the same cells and their connections. As these sounds are heard repeatedly, the neural connections become stronger and the sounds become more easily recognized or familiar. In this way, the brain also begins to distinguish between sounds that are alike and those that are different. This is a process essential to phonemic awareness. In addition, researchers have found that early knowledge of nursery rhymes is strongly and specifically related to the development of more abstract word processing skills and future reading ability (Maclean, Bryant, & Bradley, 1978).

The repetition of sounds set to a rhythm is a common memory strategy nearly everyone uses, and one of the best ways to develop word processing skills in the young child is through nursery rhymes and simple songs. "Thirty days has September," and "'i' before 'e' except after 'c,'" are two familiar examples. What works for the adult brain also works for the young child's brain. It is easier for children to remember words that are repeated in a rhyme, and they are more likely to repeat them for their own pleasure (Maclean et al., 1978). It is common to hear 3-year-olds singing songs or jingles that they have heard on television or listened to on the radio or on a compact disc.

> *Researchers have found that early knowledge of nursery rhymes is strongly and specifically related to the development of more abstract word processing skills and future reading ability.*

Why are nursery rhymes and songs so important? Children not only get hooked on listening to language, they also learn valuable language skills. While children are having fun, they are learning the patterns and rhythms of language and the way it is put together. They are increasing their vocabulary and beginning to identify sounds that are the same or different, as well as beginning to develop an awareness of syllables. These are all essential components of phonemic awareness and phonological processing. While there is no research to support it, many parents and teachers have noted that adding action to the rhymes seems to further enhance their positive effects. "Pat-a-cake" is an excellent example of action incorporated into rhyme. "Where is Thumbkin?" which uses finger play, is another.

What about television, audiotapes, and video as mechanisms for increasing language? While their effects are not inherently negative, they are not generally interactive. The experience of interacting with a caregiver is irreplaceable. Children need a sounding board as they begin to practice language. They need someone who will listen, respond, and correct. This

> *The experience of interacting with a caregiver is irreplaceable.*

is an experience television and computers cannot provide. An additional benefit from any positive verbal interaction between parent or caregiver and child is the bonding and attachment that is so critical for full emotional development.

PRECURSORS TO WRITING IN THE FIRST 3 YEARS

Reading and writing skills develop together. While children generally do not start writing letters and words until around age 4, there are many opportunities for parents and caregivers to encourage writing behaviors much earlier. Starting around the end of the first year, children can be provided with resources for drawing or coloring and be encouraged to experiment with making marks. Children can be offered a wide range of media as they express interest in drawing. Crayons, finger paints, clay, and play dough are all good materials to use indoors, while "painting" with water or drawing with chalk on sidewalks are ways to experiment outdoors. Parents also have opportunities to model or demonstrate the uses of writing by signing the child's name to a birthday card, writing an item a child wants on a grocery list, writing the date a book is due at the library on a calendar, or writing a letter to a grandparent as the child dictates.

Children pass through several stages as they develop their skills in writing. The first stage could be called *early scribbling,* where the child makes random marks on paper. Children at this stage are probably more interested in the physical experience than in what is being marked on the paper. As children's motor skills develop, the marks become more controlled, with efforts to draw a straight line or a circle. This stage could be labeled *controlled scribbling.* At this stage, some children begin to distinguish between drawing and writing. With vertical lines under a picture, the child may ask, "What did I write?" or "How do you write 'Daddy'?" The third stage might be called the *pictorial stage*, where the marks and forms begin to be distinguishable and where the child understands that pictures and words are different symbols. In the final stage, which could be labeled the *letter stage*, young children begin to write letters to

> *Children pass through several stages as they develop their skills in writing.*

represent words and syllables and often can write their own name (adapted from MacDonal, 1997). As a final summary of language and literacy development in the young child, we present the following overview of the developmental accomplishments of the child from birth to age 3. This list is taken from the National Research Council's publication *Preventing Reading Difficulties in Young Children* (Snow et al., 1998, p. 61).

recognizes specific books by cover

pretends to read books

understands that books are handled in particular ways

enters into a book-sharing routine with primary caregivers

vocalization play in crib gives way to enjoyment of rhyming language, nonsense word play, etc.

labels objects in books

comments on characters in books

looks at picture in book and realizes it is a symbol for real object

listens to stories

requests/commands adult to read or write

may begin attending to specific print such as letters in names

uses increasingly purposive scribbling

occasionally seems to distinguish between drawing and writing

produces some letter-like forms and scribbles with some features of English writing

Learning to talk is probably one of the greatest accomplishments of an individual's life. Even though the structures for language appear to be hardwired in the brain and nearly all children learn to speak, we are obviously not born speaking. In this chapter, we have seen that the first 3 years of life are a critical period for developing children's language capacity, vocabulary, and writing skills. The environmental aspects of children's lives, their experiences, whether they are read and talked to, the opportunities they have to experiment with writing, all play an important role in building a strong foundation for later reading success. In the next chapter, we'll take a look at the final years before formal schooling begins to see how we can build on the foundation of the first 3 years.

REFLECTIVE QUESTIONS

1. Explain the statement, "In a sense, learning to read begins at birth."

2. Assume that you have been asked to give a presentation to parents of young children. What suggestions would you make that will increase the probability of their children's future reading success?

3. If you are reading this book as part of a study group, ask someone to prepare a short presentation on the benefits of reading aloud to young children.

4. Define the "nursery rhyme effect" and explain its importance in helping to develop a reading brain.

5. Suppose you have parents who believe that watching *Sesame Street* or other children's television programs will best prepare their child to read. What would you say to these parents?

Emerging Literacy During the Preschool Years

4

During the preschool years, children's brains are undergoing a massive reorganization, building millions of new connections (synapses) and at the same time pruning away ones that are unused. Which synapses are kept and which ones are pruned depends largely on whether they are reinforced by experience. In a sense, the preschooler has a supercharged brain. Measurements made by Harry Chugani at Children's Hospital in Detroit show that 3-and 4-year-olds' brain cells are burning glucose at twice the rate of adult brain cells (Chugani, 1998).

What is it that is using so much energy? What is the brain doing during this period of rapid growth? The brain is literally building itself. One of the human brain's most amazing capacities is its ability to sculpt itself based on what it experiences. This is called **neuroplasticity**. Almost nowhere is this neural activity as evident as in the young brain's ability to learn and store the language or languages it hears repeatedly. Brain wave

> *One of the human brain's most amazing capacities is its ability to sculpt itself based on what it experiences.*

measurements (electroencephalograms, EEGs) show a dramatic upsurge of activity in both Broca's area and Wernicke's area, which is reflected in the preschooler's snowballing vocabulary (Diamond & Hopson, 1998). The preschooler's brain has reached a level of maturation that allows it to make great strides in language acquisition. Until around the age of 4, the language pathway of the brain is not fully functional. However, Broca's area and Wernicke's area are matured, which allows the child's brain to take language learning to a new level (Eliot, 1999).

Between the ages of 3 and 5, children make tremendous strides in their mastery of language. Their average vocabulary at age 3 is about 900 words (Bee & Mitchell, 1980). Vocabulary acquisition grows at a rapid pace thereafter. By age 5, children will have a well of between 3,000 and 8,000 words on which to draw, and it is estimated that an average 6-year-old commands about 13,000 words (Pinker, 1997). These children now speak in more complex and complicated sentences and are using language to meet their personal and social needs. They enjoy listening to and talking about the stories that are read to them, are beginning to identify familiar signs and labels, participate in rhyming games, and probably understand that print carries a message. Preschool children are also showing growth in the speech fluency they need to express ideas. Most of these children are now ready to explore what it means to be a reader and a writer.*

> Research studies have shown that the language and literacy activities of the preschool years can have a significant impact on children's ability to read during the formal years of school. (Dickinson, Cote, & Smith, 1993; Dickinson & Smith, 1994; Phillips, McCartney, & Scarr, 1987)

Whether their time is spent in a preschool or at home with parents or caregivers, these children have reached a milestone in their literacy development. The preschool years are a prime time to build increased *linguistic awareness* of the language foundation set down in the brain during the first 3 years. Research studies have shown that the language and literacy activities of the preschool years can have a significant impact on children's ability to read during the formal years of school (Dickinson, Cote, & Smith, 1993; Dickinson & Smith, 1994; Phillips, McCartney, & Scarr, 1987).

DEVELOPMENTALLY APPROPRIATE ACTIVITIES

While the preschool years are a prime time for developing the emergent reader's literacy skills, we need to emphasize that we are not advocating

---

*It is important to emphasize that while the information and activities in this chapter are designed for the preschool-aged child, there is tremendous variance in children's background experiences, their rates of maturation, and their readiness to engage in pre-reading activities. Some of the guidelines and suggested activities in this chapter will be appropriate for 3-year-olds. Other children's brains will be a bit slower to develop, and they may not be ready for the activities until perhaps age 5. The term "preschool" as used in this chapter refers to an age range (3½ to 5) rather than to children enrolled in a formal preschool program.

the "pushing down" of the kindergarten or first-grade curriculum. Unfortunately, some parents, policymakers, and educators believe that when children are not learning to read in the early grades using the standard reading curriculum and strategies, we should simply start teaching them to read earlier. This belief results in parents buying phonics workbooks for their 3- and 4-year-olds and preschools advertising "academic" programs guaranteed to teach young children to read. The belief that "earlier is better" is based on a lack of understanding of the reading process, of children's brain development, and of the types of activities that are best suited for different ages.

Language and literacy development in the preschool years should not stress isolated skills development or formal instruction in phonics. Linguistic awareness is best developed within the context of the child's work and play. The environment, whether at home or in preschool, should provide many opportunities to hear and play with language. These opportunities should, whenever possible, be a part of the child's natural experiences (Bredekamp, 1987).

The preschool child's environment is rich with opportunities to develop language and emergent literacy skills. Shopping for groceries, visiting the park, going to the library, sorting clothes for washing, or preparing a meal, all offer opportunities to build vocabulary and increase the child's understanding of concepts. Reading poems and stories, engaging in dramatic play, seeing classroom charts and other print in use, and singing rhymes are additional activities that are appropriate at this stage of development. Beginning writing skills are enhanced when children draw, color (but not within the lines), copy, and invent their own spellings (Chomsky, 1979). Given the caveat that earlier is not necessarily better, next we will take a look at some of the appropriate linguistic awareness activities that best prepare the young child for more formal literacy instruction.

> *The preschool child's environment is rich with opportunities to develop language and emergent literacy skills.*

Continuing to Build Oral Language Skills

Many of the activities that nurture literacy and language development suggested in the previous chapter for younger children continue to be appropriate for 4-year-olds, but at a somewhat more advanced level. As we noted at the beginning of this chapter, children at 4 have experienced a relatively large jump in brain development during the previous year. Their brains are now approximately 90 percent of their final adult size and weight. They have not, of course, reached the same level of functioning as an adult. These children, however, are fairly sophisticated learners. They continue to enjoy many of the language activities they engaged in at 2 and 3, but with their newly developed language and cognitive skills, they can now be expected to be more active participants.

In Chapter 3, we discussed how essential it is to talk to infants and young children and how it helps them develop an understanding of the way language is used. At the same time, it increases their brains' store of both vocabulary and concepts. At 4, most children now have the capability to engage in a dialog with adults. Every parent is more than familiar with the ubiquitous "Why?" of 3- and 4-year-olds. Sometimes adults spend time carefully answering their children's questions and miss an opportunity to engage children in a discussion of what they think the answer might be.

> *Sometimes adults spend time carefully answering their children's questions and miss an opportunity to engage children in a discussion of what they think the answer might be.*

The quality of adult-child discourse and the amount of time allotted to these interactions appear to be critical factors. The conversations need to be cognitively challenging and vocabulary-rich for literacy learning to occur (Dickinson et al., 1993). There are many avenues for language development when engaging in conversations with preschool children. Before we discuss some of these, we will review some general guidelines for these conversations.

These are conversations, not lessons. They should be natural, unobtrusive, and not dominated by the adult.

Adults should be prepared to give the child their full attention and support the child's efforts to communicate by listening patiently.

The child should control the subject of the conversation and be provided words only when needed.

Sentence structure or grammar should be corrected by modeling, not by instructing. When the child says, "I knowed that man was going to jump," the adult should respond with, "So, you knew he was going to jump."

There are many ways to enhance children's language skills during the course of normal conversation. Here are some.

Rephrase and extend the child's words. Child: "I see a doggie." Adult: "Yes, that is a special kind of dog called a Golden Retriever."

Ask a clarifying question. When the child says, "I saw a man," the adult might ask the child to describe him or tell more about him.

Model more complex vocabulary or sentence structure. Child: "I made a building." Adult: "I see you built a tall skyscraper with lots of windows so people can look out and see the city."

Ask open-ended questions. Child: "I liked that story." Adult: "What was your favorite part of the story?"

Ask "curiosity questions." During a mealtime, the adult asks, "Where do you think those potatoes came from?" Or while in the library, the adult asks, "Who do you think writes all these books?" (adapted from Hall & Moats, 1999).

In the course of reading to children, adults can further enhance the children's word awareness by pointing to individual words, directing children's attention to where to begin reading, and helping children to recognize letter shapes and sounds.

In the preschool setting, there may be children who are learning English as a second language. Many believe that these children are more likely to become readers and writers of English when they are already familiar with the vocabulary and concepts in their primary language (Clay, 1993; New York State Education Department, 2000). High-quality preschool programs recognize that these children may need different strategies and progress at varying rates. They also provide basic information to their parents as to how children acquire a first and second language (California Department of Education, 2000b).

Enhancing Comprehension Through Story Time

Being read to aloud in an expressive manner from an appealing book has been associated with improved literacy learning (Clay, 1979). The preschool child still needs and wants to be read to. However, caregivers can make reading time an opportunity to further develop two important literacy skills: print exploration and comprehension.

> Being read to aloud in an expressive manner from an appealing book has been associated with improved literacy learning.

In recent years, we have seen increasing awareness of the importance of parents and caregivers reading to children (Bus, Van Ijzendoorn, & Pellegrini, 1995; Wells, 1985). One of the major advantages of reading aloud to children is that it develops a sense of story—beginning, middle, end—a key skill for future reading and comprehension of text. Many additional functions related to future reading success are served by reading to children.

When parents and caregivers make reading enjoyable, they promote positive feelings about books and the purposes of reading.

Being read to from many different kinds of books develops children's background knowledge about a variety of topics, especially those that are not a part of their present experience.

Reading aloud to children builds their vocabulary. It creates opportunities to introduce children to new words that represent concepts with which they are unfamiliar. Explaining new words, especially when the book contains an illustration representing the words, allows children to begin to store an inventory of mental images so that the words have meaning. Remember that comprehension depends on knowing the meaning of words.

Reading to children provides an opportunity to engage them in inferential thinking. Children can be questioned as to what a character might be feeling or what they think might happen next.

As children develop familiarity with a story, they may begin to engage in "pretend" reading. Adults should listen and encourage this activity, as it is evidence that the child is beginning to understand the structure of a story and that the story is contained within the print on the page.

As the preceding list indicates, it is the talk that surrounds the reading of the book that gives it power, increasing children's vocabulary development and their understanding of the meanings of the words (Snow, Burns, & Griffin, 1998). It is enjoying the book together, reflecting on the story, asking open-ended questions, inviting discussions of the meanings of words, and supporting children's curiosity about print. Research has demonstrated that when parents are taught to engage in these types of activities when reading to their children, the children score significantly higher on tests of verbal expression and vocabulary than children of parents who read stories straight through without the activities (Whitehurst et al., 1988). Unfortunately, there are many homes where children's literacy skills are not developed in the ways mentioned previously. Lacking these experiences, many children are at a disadvantage when beginning formal reading instruction on entering school (Snow et al., 1998).

THE INTEGRAL ROLE OF PRINT AWARENESS

Print is everywhere. From cereal boxes to McDonald's signs, children are surrounded by letters combined in a myriad of ways to form thousands of words.

At some point, it is essential for children to understand the many qualities of print. In her book *Beginning to Read*, Marilyn Jager Adams outlines some of these qualities (Adams, 1990).

> Print is print no matter where it is found—on signs, on the sides of trucks, on paper, on television, on blocks and toys, or on clothing. It can be black and white or in color, but it is still print.
>
> Adults use print in many different ways—to determine the price of an item, to read a novel or a newspaper, or to label a jar of jam.
>
> Print can be produced by anyone. It can be produced with crayons, paint, a pencil, or a pen on almost any surface.
>
> Print is different from other kinds of visual information. It is distinct from pictures and other patterns.
>
> Print holds information. It holds the stories in books, gives directions on how to operate a machine or a toy, lists phone numbers in a book, indicates what time a movie starts, and tells what flavors of ice cream are available at the store.
>
> Print symbolizes language, and what we say can be written. This is perhaps the final and most important thing that children must learn about print.

In fact, children's performance on tests designed to measure print awareness predicts future reading achievement (Tunmer, Herriman, & Nesdale, 1988). If children are immersed in a print-rich environment, many, if not most, children gain this awareness on their own and do not require instruction. Even though this occurs for many children, we should not take print awareness for granted. Some children may need our help in understanding the many uses of print. At the least, we need to be more alert to print awareness, as well as all the other factors that influence a child's complex journey toward becoming a reader, and understand why exposure to many types of print enhances this journey.

> *Some children may need our help in understanding the many uses of print.*

THE ALPHABET AND RAPID LETTER NAMING

In the 1960s, several research studies reported the best predictor of beginning reading achievement to be a child's knowledge of letter names of the alphabet (Bond & Dykstra, 1967; Chall, 1967). This research was greeted with much enthusiasm, as it appeared to be a simple way to give children an advantage in learning to read. In fact, in many homes it would be difficult to find a 4-year-old who has not learned to sing the alphabet song. However, further research found that pre-readers' knowledge of the letters and their names, while a good predictor of future reading success, is not enough (Adams, 1990). Just teaching children the names of the letters of the alphabet does not help much. Researchers found that it is not just the accuracy with which children can name letters that gives them an advantage, it is the fluency or ease with which they do so (Walsh, Price, & Gillingham, 1988).

> *In the 1960s, several research studies reported the best predictor of beginning reading achievement to be a child's knowledge of letter names of the alphabet (Bond & Dykstra, 1967; Chall, 1967).*

Why are speed and accuracy of naming such critical factors? The discussion in earlier chapters regarding automaticity makes it clear. Children who do not automatically see the words as wholes will have to invest a great deal of conscious effort in order to decipher each letter, leaving little "space" in working memory for processing and remembering them. The ability to recognize most of the letters automatically will make it easier for the child to recognize patterns of letters—a key to reading words.

Word and Syllable Counting

After children have developed the ability to quickly recognize and name the letters of the alphabet and when they have learned to count objects, a natural next step is to count the words in a sentence or the syllables in a word. Words and syllables are more directly perceivable than the individual sounds of letters, making this activity more accessible than the phonemic awareness activities that follow. Word counting should be done with children listening to an adult slowly reading a sentence. They should not be looking at the print. To help them keep track of the words, they can place a marker from left to right for each word they hear. The parent or caregiver can reinforce their counting by re-reading the sentence and having the children touch each marker as a word is read.

> *Syllables can be thought of as the bridge between words and phonemes, words being easier to hear and phonemes being more difficult than syllables.*

Syllables can be thought of as the bridge between words and phonemes, words being easier to hear and phonemes being more difficult than syllables. It makes sense, then, that the ability to detect and count syllables might be more strongly related to reading acquisition than the ability to count words in sentences. And indeed it is. The ability to detect syllables in speech has been shown to predict future reading, correlates with the reading progress of beginners, and differentiates older dyslexic readers from normal first-grade readers (Lundberg, Olofsson, & Wall, 1980; Morais, Bertelson, Cary, & Alegria, 1986). For the preschool child, counting syllables in words can be a game (and use up excess energy) if children are asked to clap hands or march in place for each syllable. The adult can start with a child's two-syllable name (John-ny or Mar-cie), objects in the environment (win-dow), or a feeling (hap-py), and when the child is successful with these, advance to three-syllable words.

Phonemic Awareness

A considerable amount of research has been conducted on the importance of phonemic awareness for future reading success. A growing consensus exists that an understanding that speech is composed of individual sounds is essential for learning to read. According to Bond and Dykstra's research, an excellent predictor of first-grade reading achievement is the ability to discriminate between phonemes (Bond & Dykstra, 1967). This research is further substantiated by the finding that students with reading disabilities seem to lack phonemic awareness (Stanovich, 1998). G. Reid Lyon of the National Institute of Child Health and Human Development (NICHD) points out that the typical disabled reader cannot distinguish phonemes and states that this deficit may be one of

> *According to Bond and Dykstra's research, an excellent predictor of first-grade reading achievement is the ability to discriminate between phonemes (Bond & Dykstra, 1967).*

the causes of dyslexia among children who have "average or above average intelligence. . ." (Lyon, 2002). Children learn best through active involvement and exploration of their environment. However, research confirms that many preschool children benefit from age-appropriate explicit instruction in some areas of phonemic awareness and phonological awareness (Snow et al., 1998). Knowing that many children may benefit from explicit instruction is one thing; determining which children and what types of activities are most appropriate is another.

Before we look at these activities, it is important to review the distinction between the terms phonemic awareness and phonological awareness. As we have stated, phonemic awareness is the understanding that spoken language is made up of identifiable units. Phonological awareness is a broader umbrella term that includes phonemic awareness, but also includes more complex awareness such as counting the number of phonemes in a word, blending phonemes, or distinguishing parts of syllables called onsets and rimes.

How do we determine whether children have phonemic or phonological awareness, and if they do not, how do we teach it to them? Interestingly,

> *How do we determine whether children have phonemic or phonological awareness, and if they do not, how do we teach it to them?*

similar activities often serve both purposes. For example, children can be asked whether two words in a rhyme sound the same. If they are not able to determine this, rhyming games can be used to increase their ability to hear words that sound alike. In the following sections, the levels of phonemic and phonological awareness will be discussed along with age-appropriate activities to develop awareness and build these word processing skills.

We wish to re-emphasize that the activities to teach young children these skills should be embedded within a context of their work and play as

> *We are not recommending formal lessons or workbooks for 3- and 4-year-olds.*

much as possible. We are not recommending formal lessons or workbooks for 3- and 4-year-olds. However, children love to sing and chant nursery rhymes, and they love the challenge of the "puzzle" of figuring out the beginning sound of a word. Much learning can be accomplished within a game format with these young children.

A second consideration is the short attention span of preschool children. Even though the activity may be enjoyable, it will not be, if carried on too long. Spending a few minutes daily engaging preschool children in activities that emphasize the sound of language goes a long way toward enhancing their future success as readers (Honig, 2001).

In a preschool class, some children, because of previous experiences in their homes, will have more phonemic awareness than others. In fact, some children acquire phonemic awareness skills without specific training. It is probably not necessary to do a formal assessment and differentiate instruction for children at this age. All will enjoy and benefit from the same activities if appropriately designed and implemented.

Developmental Levels of Phonemic Awareness

In her book *Beginning to Read,* Marilyn Jager Adams (1990) describes five levels of phonemic awareness, two of which will be discussed in the following section. Note that there is not complete agreement in the literature as to the appropriateness of phonemic awareness activities for preschool children. In the position statement of the International Reading Association (IRA) and the National Association for the Education of Young Children (NAEYC), the authors state, "Although children's facility in phonemic awareness has been shown to be strongly related to later reading achievement, the precise role it plays in these early years is not fully understood" (National Association for the Education of Young Children, 1998). This issue may be more a matter of semantics than a disagreement about whether children should be involved in phonemic awareness activities.

While Adams calls rhyming and oddity tasks phonemic awareness activities, the authors of the position paper label them linguistic awareness activities. We would agree with the latter position, viewing the following activities, as well as the ones that have been discussed earlier in this chapter, as precursors to phonemic awareness that might more accurately be called linguistic awareness.

Rhyming

According to Adams, the simplest or most primitive level of phonemic awareness involves not much more than an ear for the sound of words and the ability to hear rhymes and alliteration. As was pointed out in Chapter 3, teaching nursery rhymes is one of the easiest and most effective ways to increase a child's ability to hear the similar sounds of rhyming words (Adams, 1990). Recall also that the pattern of words in a rhyme or song appear to be stored in implicit or unconscious memory, and are easily brought to conscious memory as a whole.

> *The simplest or most primitive level of phonemic awareness involves not much more than an ear for the sound of words and the ability to hear rhymes and alliteration.*

Think about the endings to the phrases, "i" before "e" except _____, or, When two vowels go walking, _____. The unconscious part of the brain remembers the rest of the phrases without conscious processing.

The word "rhyme" can be introduced at this point, and parents and caregivers can make a game out of finding words that rhyme. Alliteration activities can also be an effective strategy to increase a child's ear for words. Playing with their friends' names—Happy Henry or Merry Megan—or tongue twisters, such as Peter Piper picked a peck of pickled peppers, are fun ways to introduce preschoolers to alliteration and increase their ability to distinguish between similar and different phonemes at the beginning of words.

One natural and spontaneous way to work with children on rhymes and alliteration is to focus on literature that deals playfully with speech sounds through rhymes such as the Dr. Seuss book *There's a Wocket in My Pocket* (Seuss, 1974) or *Moses Supposes His Toeses Are Roses* (Patz, 1983). Yopp (1985) provides guidelines for using these books with children: (a) read and re-read the stories; (b) comment on the use of language; (c) encourage predictions of sound and word patterns; (d) comment on or elicit specific aspects of sound patterns (e.g., "What sound do you hear at the beginning of all those words?"); and (e) be creative in inventing new versions of the language patterns utilized in the stories. Adding music to the mix often enhances the effectiveness of rhyming and alliteration. Young children have an amazing capacity to remember the tunes and words of nursery rhymes and songs

> *Young children have an amazing capacity to remember the tunes and words of nursery rhymes and songs they've been taught.*

they've been taught. Most preschool teachers can attest to their children's desire to sing familiar songs over and over.

Some children struggle to hear rhymed words and may need more specific instruction. Rhyme recognition can be reinforced by direct modeling of instances (mat-cat) and noninstances (bed-car). Children are then presented with other pairs and asked if the two words sound the same or different. This can be made into a game using happy face cards for words that rhyme and a sad face for those that don't.

Oddity Tasks

The next level of phonemic awareness requires children to compare the sounds, determining whether they are the same or different. Orally presenting children with two or three words that rhyme, and one that doesn't, the adult asks them to tell which one doesn't belong (cat, hat, mouse, bat). Or the child may be presented with two or three words that begin the same and one that begins with a different sound (pig, pen, hat, pie). Another more difficult oddity task asks children to make their decision based on the ending sound (dog, hill, pill) or the middle sound in a word (man, fun, bun). These oddity tasks have proved especially usable with pre-readers, as they do not require children to decompose a syllable into a string of individual phonemes or blend sounds (Adams, 1990).

The additional levels of phonemic awareness described by Adams (blending and syllable splitting, phoneme segmentation tasks, and phoneme manipulation tasks) will be addressed in the next chapter under phonological processing. Although some 4-year-olds may have the ability to engage in some of these more advanced phonemic awareness activities (e.g., changing the first letter in a word to make a new word or blending or isolating initial/medial sounds in a word), most are not appropriate for the developmental level of preschool children. Parents and caregivers must allow for and be prepared for individual differences in children and make certain that, whatever the activity, its tone is one of fun and informality.

THE DEVELOPING WRITING
SKILLS OF THE PRESCHOOL CHILD

Being able to express thoughts and ideas in writing is an essential component of literacy. Throughout the earlier chapters, we have emphasized the development of oral language vocabulary as an important factor in future reading success. Research has also found that this vocabulary is essential for the development of young children's written vocabulary (Snow & Tabors, 1993). Children not only need to be immersed in a print- and language-enriched environment, they also need to be exposed and have opportunities to begin to express themselves in writing.

As preschool children's fine-motor control increases, many begin to experiment with writing in various forms and as they do this they are literally making neural connections in the motor cortex. However, developmentally, preschool children exhibit a wide range of readiness for writing, and adults who work with these children should be aware of the variance. However, all children can be provided with opportunities to write and should be encouraged to write when they begin to express interest. A print-rich environment can greatly enhance children's understanding of writing. In addition to reading to children, adults can print letters on artwork, label toy shelves with pictures and words that describe objects, write children's names on birthday cards, and write on a grocery list items that are needed for a meal.

Scribbling is one of the earliest forms of writing in which young children engage. In homes or schools where children observe adults writing for different purposes, children will often mimic the adults by making marks on a paper and then ask adults what their "writing" says. Adults should not expect a representational product. These attempts at writing are an exploration of print (Bredekamp, 1987). This occurs more readily when children are provided with the proper tools for writing and various opportunities to write. Many preschool classrooms have a writing center, a post office, a restaurant with order pads, or a doctor's office with prescription pads where children can engage in pretend writing.

Teachers and parents can demonstrate the use of writing by serving as scribes and helping children write down their ideas or describe their artwork. Adults who work with preschool children need to keep in mind the balance between children doing their own "writing" and doing it for them. In the beginning, children are often more interested in what they have drawn or painted than in writing letters or words. However, with encouragement, children begin to attempt to label their pictures or write their own stories.

As preschool children begin to write, they often use their tacit knowledge of word sounds to spell the words, usually called *invented spelling* (or phonic spelling). Beginning writers often use the symbols they associate with the sounds of the letters they want to write (e.g., "lk" for like or "bcz" for because). Some educators and parents have worried that invented spelling promotes poor spelling habits. The research indicates quite the contrary. Studies suggest that *temporary* invented spelling may contribute to better reading and that children benefit from using invented spelling compared to having the teacher provide correct spellings (Clarke, 1988).

In summarizing the emerging literacy skills of the preschool child, the joint National Association for the Education of Young Children/International Reading Association position paper states:

> Thus the picture that emerges from research in these first years of children's reading and writing is one that emphasizes wide exposure to print and to developing concepts about it and its forms and functions. (National Association for the Education of Young Children, 1998)

Homes and preschool classrooms filled with print, language play, reading of stories, and writing allow children to experience reading as a joyous and powerful experience, while mastering the basic concepts about print that research has shown to be strong predictors of future reading success. In sum, remembering that the brain builds itself through its experience helps us to understand the role that parents and caregivers have in enhancing children's language skills. No matter what their genetic potential, all children can benefit from a positive language environment, less TV, and more reading and conversation (Eliot, 1999).

REFLECTIVE QUESTIONS

1. What is the benefit of holding conversations with preschool children and what are some of the guidelines for these conversations?

2. Prepare an outline for a presentation to parents about how they can make story time a more productive experience for their children.

3. Explain what print awareness is and its role in emerging literacy.

4. If you are reading this book as part of a study group, be ready to discuss phonemic awareness, why it is important, how it develops and what educators need to do to help parents understand their role in developing it in their children.

5. Explain the phonemic awareness activities, oddity tasks, and rhyming and explain how they influence emerging reading skills.

Beginning to Read   5

Ages 5 and 6

Kindergarten marks the beginning of a core transition in the life of young learners. Children arrive at kindergarten with tremendous variation in their maturity and pre-reading foundation. Despite a range of exposure to print, variation in vocabulary, understanding of story structure, and other foundation pre-reading skills, all children are expected to transition from pre-readers to readers during their first 2 years in a formal, structured classroom. What will happen in the brains of these 5- and 6-year-old children during these years as they are learning to read?

Neuroscientists have shown that different structures of the brain are activated as children learn and practice the new skills that they will need in a literate world. Although a great deal of brain development occurs in the preschool years, neurons (nerve cells) in the brain continue the process of making connections and forming networks to store and assimilate information and concepts that the child is learning in primary school. Teachers who are aware of these changes can provide activities that help to structure this neural development.

ELEMENTS OF INSTRUCTION FOR EMERGING READERS

In recent years, states and the federal government have worked to define curriculum standards that will promote success in reading. Research-based guidelines and standards for reading and language arts identify specific information, concepts, and skills for children to master at each grade level. Reading First is the portion of the federal government's No Child Left Behind Act that specifically identifies five components for effective reading. These components are phonemic awareness, phonics, reading fluency, vocabulary development, and reading comprehension. We will discuss all these elements in this book, but we have modified this list by adding one new component and combining several of the Reading First components. The areas that we will address are:

priming skills

decoding

comprehension

fluency

Two elements considered to be priming skills, attention and memory, were previously introduced in Chapter 2. These elements are basic to the other priming skills of motivation, concentration, and organization. Teachers can assess these skill areas as they observe their students' work behaviors and concentrate on the quality of answers children provide. Because attention and memory are so vital, teachers need to clearly understand these factors and support their development.

Learning to Pay Attention

As we previously discussed, many parts of the brain must work together for children to become fluent readers. However, the ability to pay attention underlies the accomplishment of all reading tasks. Berninger and Richards, professors of neuropsychology and neuroscience, respectively, at the University of Washington, describe the maintenance of attention as a job for the frontal lobes, as the reader seeks to interpret and identify meaningful

> . . . the majority of the signals were not only detained, but also dropped from memory as if the input were never received.

words (Berninger & Richards, 2002). How is a child able to attend during the complex process of interpreting print when the task is complicated and there are so many distractions in the classroom?

In an intriguing study conducted at the Berlin NeuroImaging Center, Blankenburg and a team of researchers (Blankenburg et al., 2003) used functional magnetic resonance imaging (fMRI) to monitor brain activities. They intentionally produced unimportant, irrelevant stimulation, and then looked at images to determine what the brain did to inhibit the unnecessary signals.

According to Blankenburg and his colleagues, certain brain cells are called *inhibitory neurons.* The task for these neurons is to screen out many of the unimportant sensory signals when they reach the brain's thalamus, a structure in the primitive part of the brain for relaying sensory input. This study found that the majority of the signals were not only detained, but also dropped from memory as if the input were never received. This process appears to free the cerebral cortex to focus attention on the specific sensory information that is the most relevant to the individual task at hand (Blankenburg et al., 2003).

Because children's brains appear to automatically filter incoming stimuli, they may need prompts to attend specifically to a reading task. The reading brain is challenged to perceive visual symbols, interpret them, and determine if they are identifiable with words that are already known. Psychologist Franklin Manis (2003) of the University of Southern California refers to a focused, complex process that occurs in the brains of successful readers as they process letter distinctions fast enough to maintain the flow and fluency of the text (Ackerman, 2003). If the perceived letters or string of words is unfamiliar or appears to have no meaning, the process slows down or stalls. It is then the job of the frontal lobes to help determine if the visual input is important enough for the child to maintain attention (Berninger & Richards, 2002). The complexities of maintaining attention to identify and learn sounds don't happen for most children without practice.

> *Because children's brains appear to automatically filter incoming stimuli, they may need prompts to attend specifically to a reading task.*

Attending to Task

In school, children receive a multitude of sensory input from the classroom environment, and some 5- and 6-year-olds need help developing the kind of selective attention that school demands. There are external noises—children moving, papers shuffling, a cough, a truck driving by outside—and there are internal signals from the child's own body indicating hunger, thirst, or a feeling of being too hot or cold. Learning to read demands attention to specific sensory input, such as a teacher's signal or a written prompt, while ignoring irrelevant sensory information. Teachers need to provide various prompts for young learners to develop the habit of focusing on the relevant instructional stimuli.

Teachers can help focus students' attention to task by shifting activities among instructional formats, such as by moving from teacher input to hands-on activities, individual seatwork, learning centers, or by requiring active engagement from the students. Varying amounts of time can be devoted to different activities, depending on the difficulty of the task or the amount of motivation that the task requires from the children.

Sustained attention for a lesson on sound-symbol relationships might last a tightly focused 10 to 20 minutes. Highly motivating, hands-on activities of writing letters in a tray of sand or using colored markers on wipe-off boards may sustain children's attention longer. In addition to varying the length of instructional periods, kindergarten and first-grade teachers may schedule "brain breaks" with quiet time, large motor activities, songs, or games to rejuvenate mental energy (Levine, 2003).

Getting Set to Listen

Effective teachers use varying attention-focusing strategies for classroom management to help children develop the habit of following directions. Prompts may be specific directions such as "Stop what you are doing." "Put down whatever is in your hands." "Look at me." or "Return to your desks." In each case, a finite amount of time is allowed for children to transition from an active task to focused attention and to then be ready to listen. A signal, such as the teacher raising five fingers one at a time with the expectation that children will give full attention by the time that all five fingers are visible, reinforces required behaviors.

Teachers who prepare children for transition activities—to get ready to work, to listen, to go outside, or to clean up—model expectations and help the brain to disengage from one activity and prepare for the next. In the same way, teachers can prepare students to pay attention to peers when they expect them to show attending behavior for listening. In the classroom, the key points for active listening can be identified, practiced, and posted. The rules might look like this:

One person talks at a time.

Look at the person who is talking.

Wait to raise your hand until the other person is finished talking. (Hamaguchi, 2000)

Candice Goldsworthy, professor and department vice-chairperson at California State University at Sacramento, suggests prompting children through "vigilance, focused listening and looking" with a variety of teacher-directed activities (Goldsworthy, 1996, p. 135). To employ this type of practice, children are asked to listen for specific words within a list or a story read by the teacher. During this activity, children who

> . . . children who are easily distracted may need to be alerted or refocused with "Ready?" or "Get Ready!"

are easily distracted may need to be alerted or refocused with "Ready?" or "Get Ready!" Children can respond to the chosen word in a variety of ways. If the word is "tree," they could hold up a cutout of a tree each time they heard the word. Other possible responses include clapping, raising a hand, or making a tally mark on a piece of paper. Listening for sounds or strings of words are other "getting set to listen" activities.

Getting Set to Look

A "get set to look" strategy prepares children to focus on visual cuing. Students are directed to find hidden pictures, shapes, or words in a variety of materials. As children begin to identify words, word search activities that prompt children to find hidden words in columns and rows of random letters help them look for visual differences in letter sequences. Other visual cuing activities are matching patterns, pictures, letters, or words. Puzzles also provide practice for children to attend to visual cues. All these activities are a natural part of early education programs. Although many children come to school with competence for attending to visual prompts, it is important that teachers identify children who need additional practice to be able to focus attention on visual stimuli.

> *Although many children come to school with competence for attending to visual prompts, it is important that teachers identify children who need additional practice to be able to focus attention on visual stimuli.*

THE BRAIN'S MEMORY SYSTEMS

Learning to pay attention is one skill that underlies the essential elements of reading instruction. Another is the development of permanent memory storage for information, concepts, and skills necessary to become a competent reader. Functional memory accesses three systems: sensory memory, working memory, and long-term memory (Figure 2.5, p. 30). First, let us briefly review the brain's memory systems.

The five senses are always receiving information, and as discussed earlier in this chapter, we know that only a small amount of the massive information being transmitted by all of the senses is selected as important for the task of reading. Input from sensory memory is then moved into working memory. Once in working memory, the information will remain available for up to 18 seconds (McGee & Wilson, 1984).

To maintain information for a longer period, the brain uses an articulatory loop as it holds information in working memory for rehearsal. Rehearsal or practice of this type engages the brain in subvocalization, a conscious process of repeating the string of words to be remembered over and over. Thus, the

18-second limit can be extended for the targeted material. With enough practice, the information, concept, or skill becomes available for recall or demonstration from long-term memory. One important aspect of carefully controlled reading instruction and practice activities is to help students to hold relevant sensory input in working memory and practice that material until it can be recalled automatically from long-term memory.

Teachers can design classroom activities to help children consciously practice and manipulate information essential to success in reading. For example, children practice and manipulate material in working memory whenever the teacher has them work with specific letters. Consonant blends such as /pl/ are used as first-grade children become proficient in working with consonant-vowel-consonant configurations. Children are first asked to say the blend, then to say words that have this sound. Seeking and discovering other words with this sound, using the words in spoken or written sentences, and seeing words with /pl/ on their spelling list are other typical classroom activities that reinforce the blend in memory.

> *Teachers can design classroom activities to help children consciously practice and manipulate information essential to success in reading.*

Rehearsal of information is a function of working memory. It appears to reside in multiple areas of the brain, depending on the task the reader is attempting. For written language, children store the same item in multiple ways. It may be practiced in memory with codes for its orthographic word form, phonological properties, semantics, and morphological structure (Berninger & Richards, 2002). Regardless of the storage location, neuroscientists using fMRI imaging techniques have noted that as tasks become more complex, they are likely to be managed and finalized through activity in the frontal lobes (Wolfe, 2001).

Long-Term Memory Systems

The goal of rehearsing and manipulating information in working memory is to move it into long-term memory for permanent recall and use. To plan instruction that matches the brain's memory functions, teachers must understand how long-term memory functions. We will focus next on the two functional systems that the brain uses to store long-term memories for reading development: declarative (explicit) and nondeclarative (implicit) memory.

Declarative (Explicit) Memory

Declarative memory allows children to store information and to subsequently recall it by speaking or writing. To access declarative memory, most likely the child thinks consciously about the subject; has a quick, internal mental discussion about its attributes; and makes an overt response. Memo-ries stored in the brain's declarative long-term system are factual, labeling, and location types of memories that are recalled consciously. The brain calls on the hippocampus to identify a cate-gory, while the cortex, particularly the temporal lobes, provides the collec-tion of stored information (Sylwester, 1995). Information stored in long-term declarative memory uses two very distinct memory processes: semantic and episodic.

> *To access declarative memory, most likely the child thinks con-sciously about the subject; has a quick, internal mental discussion about its attributes; and makes an overt response.*

Semantic Memory. When children practice spelling words, they are working to get the information into semantic long-term memory. When they complete worksheets that match definitions with words, they are reinforcing learning for semantic memory. Likewise, using blocks or letters to represent sounds in words during phonemic manipulation provides practice for this type of memory. Some reading concepts that competent readers hold in semantic memory include phonological rules, syntax, and semantics for language; spelling patterns; and word meanings. In each case, the child can declare or use written means to tell what is known from memory.

Classroom activities should be designed so that children can master infor-mation or concepts and store them in semantic long-term memory. Teachers may be surprised at the variety of ways they support their students in learning materials that ultimately will reside in semantic long-term memory. To clarify those activities, think about reading tasks designed for practice, rehearsal, prompting, organizing, reciting, writing, and sequencing (Table 5.1). As children sort a list of words into categories with phoneme labels, what is the memory goal? They are developing organizational patterns of sounds to be stored in declarative semantic memory.

Episodic Memory. While lessons are strategically planned for children to prac-tice and manipulate information for semantic memory, many experiences that are recorded in episodic memory happen by chance. A child who witnesses the family dog giving birth to puppies will have strong memories about that unusual experience. The event and the child's opportunity to experience it were not necessarily planned. However, such experiences, due to their extreme emo-tional nature, allow the brain to effortlessly move details of the event into long-term episodic memory. Accessing long-term memory for needed reading skill development using episodic experiences is powerful but challenging. Teachers

Table 5.1   Declarative Semantic Memory Strategies

Process	Teacher Directions	Student Response
Practice	Put your spelling words on flash cards to self-check.	Writes, spells, and sorts words.
Rehearsal	Say the rules and match three words for each.	Reviews rules and shows understanding.
Prompting	It begins like "bubble."	Selects word from a list.
Organizing	Put your words in groups that begin with the same sound.	Makes a chart that organizes words into groups with the same beginning sound.
Reciting	Look at the word and say the rule.	Reviews the word list for orthographic rules.
Writing	Write the words as I say them.	Listens to sounds and attaches graphemes.
Sequencing	Put these words for the days of the week in order.	Sorts and orders word cards.

can help children access prior experiences with broad prompts or questions about locale or the core experience from a reading selection, such as "Think about a time when you went to an exciting place you'd never been before." Teachers need to be careful, however, about asking questions that may tap traumatic experiences, such as "Were you ever bullied?" or "Think of a time when you were afraid." Because of the uncertainty of what children may remember, accessing prior knowledge through episodic memory is less likely to be a part of the school experience. However, planning high-impact activities is recommended as part of instructional planning for reading.

> *While lessons are strategically planned for children to practice and manipulate information for semantic memory, many experiences that are recorded in episodic memory happen by chance.*

Picture a first-grade classroom where the children are involved in a classic Winnie the Pooh story. Pooh eats too much honey and cannot get out of Rabbit's front door. The children act out the story by pretending that a chair with an open back is Rabbit's door. Christopher Robin and all of Pooh's friends are on one side of the chair. Rabbit is on the other, and Pooh is stuck halfway in and halfway out of the chair as the story play proceeds. What will children remember from this experience?

What children remember from an episodic activity depends on each child's needs and interests and on what the teacher emphasizes after the activity is complete. This story play contains action and emotion for the children who are

Table 5.2   Declarative Episodic Memory Strategies

Strategy	Learning Event	Student Involvement
Experience	Taking a field trip	Firsthand sensory stimuli
Elaboration	Describing how the subject may have looked and acted when he/she arrived at school	Expanding conceptual understanding by picturing and identifying new details
Story Play	Reading or acting out a story	Active engagement or active attention to peers
Role Playing	Pretending to be the character or person named on a card	Active engagement from another's perception
Demonstration	Showing a story or details from informative text on a flannel board or chart	Heightened attention due to novelty of presentation

role-playing and for their classmates who are watching. Students may learn vocabulary, the sequence of the story, a lesson about eating too much, more about the story's meaning and structure, or that reading stories is fun.

Children record an experience such as this one in episodic long-term memory. This type of declarative memory is called **source memory**. The power of the emotional attributes of the experience allows children—as well as adults—to recall what happened, where it happened, and when it happened (Wolfe, 2001). Teachers prompt episodic memory when they plan activities that provide experience, elaboration, story plays, role-playing, or demonstration (see Table 5.2).

An episodic experience is a quick, active way to get information into long-term memory, but it is not always accurate. Experience tells us that as the Pooh story is retold, it is enhanced or refabricated with plot and detail additions and omissions. The details become less clear and often become distorted with each recall. We experience this phenomenon when adults retell a joke. Each time the humorous situation is repeated the details become less like the original version. Likewise, children will form their own individual long-term memories of the episodic experience. If they talk about the experience at home, chances are strong that they will each have a unique way of describing what they remember and what seemed most interesting to them.

If, however, the teacher structures discussion or emphasizes concepts from lesson objectives following the story play, children focus less on the action of the story and more on abstract concepts (Sylwester, 1995). For example, the teacher may ask, "What words can you think of that describe how Pooh must have felt?" Alternatively, children may develop what they see as an applicable truth from the story, such as the need to plan ahead or to avoid overeating. Pairs of students could work together to use vocabulary from the story in new ways. Activities of this type help children to move one type of declarative long-term memory experience, episodic, into the semantic memory system.

Nondeclarative (Implicit) Memory

While semantic and episodic declarative memory stores the "what" part of memories, "how" something is done is stored in nondeclarative or implicit memory. Nondeclarative memory consists of habits and skills that have been practiced to the point that they can be performed automatically without conscious thought. As applied to reading, an example of nondeclarative memory is the rapid, automatic decoding of words. Fluent readers decode words almost effortlessly below the level of conscious thought, allowing the reading brain to consciously focus on their

> *Nondeclarative memory consists of habits and skills that have been practiced to the point that they can be performed automatically without conscious thought.*

meaning. Other examples of nondeclarative memory for cognitive tasks related to reading include talking and writing in sentences, using correct syntax, turning the pages of a book, or scanning the lines of print.

Children do not begin reading complete sentences with automatic fluency and comprehension. Some of the skills they must master before arriving at reading sentences include concepts of print, alphabetic awareness, word concept awareness, phonemic processing, word attack skills, rapid processing, skilled eye movements, development of a written vocabulary, phrase understanding, and world knowledge or experience. Classroom activities that turn the individual reading attributes of decoding, comprehending, and reading with fluency into an automatic procedure include re-reading stories, practicing sight words, rapid decoding of new or nonsense words, and other rehearsal-type strategies defined for the articulatory loop that are used for semantic long-term memory. The difference between declarative and nondeclarative memory is that when skills are mastered in nondeclarative memory, they are automatically and unconsciously performed, reducing the cognitive load as discussed in Chapter 2.

Teachers who understand what children must do to move skills for reading into automatic, implicit long-term memory can design instructional strategies to help their students become more skilled readers. Some instructional strategies that prepare children to read with implicit automaticity are repetition, practice, priming, experience, and demonstration (see Table 5.3).

It is not necessary for teachers to identify specific memory categories, such as semantic or episodic declarative memory. However, an understanding of the

Table 5.3   Nondeclarative Memory Strategies

Strategy	Learning Activity	Student Response
Repetition	Passage re-reading.	Students read, then record time and accuracy.
Practice	Read along.	Teacher reads, teacher and students read together, students read silently, and students read out loud.
Priming	Teacher presents and discusses new words before students encounter them in text.	Students read text consistently without interruptions for new words.
Experience	Students listen to and have conversation about a story read in its entirety.	Students converse about story contents, then read the story on their own.
Demonstration	Teacher reads a passage with expression.	Children practice various passages for reading with expression.

functions of sensory memory, working memory, and long-term memory are a helpful guide for teachers in structuring classroom activities. Teachers who understand that learning is measured by what children can retrieve from long-term memory are more likely to select instructional practices that engage children in memory-enhancing activities.

PRIMING SKILLS FOR 5- AND 6-YEAR-OLDS

We view the attainment of priming skills as essential support for the child's developing language-to-literacy transition. These priming skills are not to be confused with readiness skills that were a topic for educators during the 1980s.

The late Dr. Jeanne Chall (1983) provided discussion of readiness in her classic book, *Learning to Read: The Great Debate*. At that time, some educators advocated readiness activities for children who were not ready for direct reading instruction, while others argued for all children to begin reading instruction immediately upon starting school (Chall, 1983). In this book, we look at what is needed for children's brains to categorize and store information needed for reading. The skills we refer to as priming skills—the ability to pay attention and access memory, motivation, concentration, and

> *We view the attainment of priming skills as essential support for the child's developing language-to-literacy transition.*

organization—are all brain-related developments that can be integrated within the context of beginning reading instruction.

Motivation and Energy for Learning to Read

Many school-aged children have already developed motivation to read by the time they arrive at school. Still, teachers find that some children may not be equipped with necessary motivation to do the hard brainwork that is required. It takes great amounts of energy for a child to concentrate on reading preparation tasks, even in the best of circumstances. When we consider the amount of mental energy that is required to decode and read, some children may be energy challenged. In fact, although the brain is only about 5 percent of the young child's total body weight, it often uses 20 to 25 percent of all the energy available to the body (Wolfe, 2001). Teachers should be alert to the amount of mental effort required when children are asked to perform activities that are difficult or not particularly interesting. A child with a normal amount of energy can focus on a task, even if it is considered boring. A child who is tired or has a low glucose (blood sugar) level—possibly from beginning the school day without breakfast—may lack motivation to do a task or may be unable to maintain attention and concentrate sufficiently to complete the work. Recognizing that children have different levels of interest in reading and varying amounts of energy that they can devote to a reading task, teachers can plan lessons that capture the students' interest and sustain and direct their energy toward the reading activity. Additionally, they can structure instruction and practice activities in appropriate time blocks to match the energy levels of their students.

> *A child who is tired or has a low glucose (blood sugar) level—possibly from beginning the school day without breakfast—may lack motivation to do a task or may be unable to maintain attention and concentrate sufficiently to complete the work.*

Concentration

Concentration is the ability to attend to information over an extended time. Some children have particular problems concentrating long enough to maintain the names of objects or words in working memory. Liberman and her research colleagues report that in children with this type of deficit is generally associated only with linguistic objects. The impairment, which is noticeable in some, but not all, children who are poor readers, is specific to reading attributes. It does not appear to be an all-embracing memory problem, since the same reading-challenged children showed no deficit in remembering nonsense shapes or unfamiliar faces (Liberman, Shankweiler, & Liberman, 1999).

Teachers can help all children extend the length of time they are able to concentrate on a task with instructionally designed practice. During reading instruction, additional activities for concentration include exercises such as "Remember the words I am saying and give them back to your study partner." Or, "Think of three words that end like 'bear.' When I give the signal, partner A will tell the words to partner B." Notice that children are not asked to write the responses. Adding the requirement to write will draw on an additional brain structure, including the motor cortex, and add to the complexity of the task. Concentrated retrieval from working memory might be blocked by the additional task of writing.

> *Some children have particular problems concentrating long enough to maintain the names of objects or words in working memory.*

Other opportunities for extending concentration occur when the teacher gives directions and then pauses before children execute the command, for example, "When I say 'ready,' you can number your paper from 1 to 10." Or the teacher might say, "Pass your paper to the front of the room when I hold up both hands." The prompt is given, "Hold these words in your mind until I say go, then call them out in a normal voice." This is most successful when the teacher selects words that are meaningful for students and form clusters, such as four hamburger toppings, "ketchup, relish, mustard, tomatoes"; or zoo animals, "tiger, elephant, giraffe, anteater"; or weather, "rainy, sunny, cold, warm." This practice can be expanded by allowing student volunteers to supply four words when the teacher gives the cue. This type of practice forces students to concentrate on information held in working memory. Concentration skills are strengthened when children are required to wait before they respond to a prompt. The same direction and wait process can be applied to question and answer activities.

Another way teachers improve students' concentration is by providing practice at following directions with two or more steps. Students are prompted to concentrate as teachers intentionally give multilevel directions. This practice extends the level of difficulty beyond stating a series of simple directions. It would sound like, "Before you place your name on your paper, open your book to page 7." Or, "You will need two pieces of paper. Place one of the pieces between pages 20 and 21 in your spelling book, and keep the other paper on the top of your desk." Purposeful simulations of distracting conditions also provide powerful cognitive preparation for classroom environments during the early school years and beyond.

> *Purposeful simulations of distracting conditions also provide powerful cognitive preparation for classroom environments during the early school years and beyond.*

Organization

The priming skill of organization prepares emergent readers in two ways: to be able to readily access information in the brain and to seek order in their physical environment. Often children need help to organize their thinking. Organizational prompts offered by teachers or other adults can help children learn to label and group common concepts, and link to previously stored information. At school, teachers can use mind-mapping strategies that reflect the way the brain sorts information into categories (represented by neural networks) that will ultimately help students manipulate and recall the information. For example, if students are studying arachnids, they might start with spiders as one type of arachnid.

To use a mind-mapping strategy, the teacher writes "spider" in the middle of the chalkboard. Then the teacher makes certain that all children have had previous experience with spiders. If not, actual spiders or pictures of spiders can be introduced to establish an initial knowledge base. The teacher can also find out what is already in the children's knowledge base by asking what they know about spiders and recording their responses. This information could be organized under the heading, "What We Know." Then children are asked what questions they have about spiders. The teacher records their responses with a heading such as "What We Want to Know" (Ogle, 1986). This frequently used technique strengthens existing neural networks and develops new connections to be used for storage of information about spiders. It allows the teacher to check for students' previous knowledge and experience and to correct misconceptions, such as a belief that spiders are insects. It also provides direction for the continued study of spiders and other arachnids. Through experiences such as mind mapping, children put conscious effort toward ordered thinking. When teachers provide activities that prime students for success in reading, students acquire self-assurance that they have the background they need to be successful with the next reading assignment.

In addition to needing structured prompts to help organize their thinking, children often need help to organize their materials and physical workspace. At home, parents can encourage students to take an initial look through an entire school assignment before they begin to work. This allows them to collect the materials they need and ask questions before they begin to work. Children often find it easier to be organized when they have a special place to work. Families who plan a work area that has good light, contains materials to complete school work, and is relatively quiet help their children to develop an organized approach to school work.

> *In addition to needing structured prompts to organize their thinking, children often need help to organize their materials and physical workspace.*

Children also need to know before they start their work at school or at home how they will know that they are finished and what to do when the task is done. Self-prompted questions might be, "What will my work look like when I am finished?" "Where do I put the completed work?" "What happens for clean up?" or "Where are school materials kept when they are not being used?" Students can learn, even at an early age, to have an internal dialogue to organize their task, assess what materials are necessary, direct their thinking toward a work strategy, and be clear about what to do when they complete the assignment.

Teacher's and Student's Work

Sue Bredekamp and Teresa Rosegrant describe a cycle of learning and teaching. What teachers do—*create, provide, describe, help, and guide*—and what children do—*become aware, explore, inquire, and utilize*—define teaching and learning activities that surround each new learning task (Bredekamp & Rosegrant, 1992). Children apply skills of attention, concentration, and engagement when they are exposed to a rich variety of reading and language arts activities. They draw on long-term memory to recall facts, details, and concepts. In first grade, for example, a folktale can be expanded with instructional activities that go far beyond vocabulary and reading, to include phonics, spelling, writing, science, and art. Broad thematic exposure through integrated-subject teaching is brain-compatible teaching that corrals students' attention, stimulates their engagement as learners, and provides real-life experiences as hooks for active remembering.

Learning to read is so important in the primary grades and beyond that a significant portion of the school day needs to be available for reading instruction and language arts. Richard Allington (2001) suggests that more time for reading instruction be reclaimed from noninstructional duties in a schoolwide plan for reading:

> All teachers must understand the enormous benefits that enhancing the volume of reading will provide. In such a plan there would be long blocks of uninterrupted time for reading and writing. Reading and writing would be integrated across all subject areas and a curriculum that featured wide reading and writing of informational texts as well as narratives would frame the lessons and activities. (Allington, 2001, p. 43)

Time for activities is secured by having other content areas, such as social studies, science, and, at times, math, embedded within the language arts schedule. In the primary grades, schools could allocate as much as 2½ hours of time for reading-based activities and protect this period from interruptions, such as student pullouts. Devoting a major portion of the school day for early literacy development is a recommended practice and is responsive to the rigorous demands of most state-based guidelines. More important, the brain is prompted to sort, combine, and organize information for recall from several overlapping content areas.

> *More important, the brain is prompted to sort, combine, and organize information for recall from several overlapping content areas.*

Parents' Work

During the early years of formal schooling, parents continue to play a vital role in supporting the development of literacy. It is of primary importance for parents to support reading development during elementary school by continuing to engage in the pleasure of reading and having conversations with their children, sharing language play, making library trips, telling stories, and enjoying active, playful reading together. Reading books with their children and making it a pleasurable experience is the best help parents can give to support the development of their children as readers.

As they collaborate with the school, parents can also support:

Concentration: by giving children a quiet place without distractions to read and do school papers. Later this will evolve into a homework space.

Organization: by establishing family routines that provide sufficient time for reading and other school-related tasks. Children can be helped to sort and place their school-type tools, toys, and clothes in places where they are easily found.

Motivation: by showing interest in their child's classroom progress and school activities. Posting notes from school, "refrigerator art," and "papers-to-be-proud-of" encourages and supports children to maintain a positive school attitude.

Consistency: by becoming familiar with classroom learning games and teacher expectations and incorporating the same or similar activities at home.

Attention: by helping children to remember to listen and respond to parents when they talk with them or give directions. Parents can provide prompts at home to support the habit of attention.

It is clear that children are expected to learn to read in the early grades. By the end of first grade, most parents already know if their child is on the way to becoming a fluent, competent reader, or if there will be struggles in the years to come.

The end-of-the-year first-grade classroom, as a product of the teacher's, students', and parents' work, looks very different from the classroom on the opening day of kindergarten. The classroom provides evidence of serious work with literacy while books and print appear in abundance. Content areas of writing, spelling, penmanship, mathematics, social studies, and science fold into instruction that matches the overarching need for children to become fluent, competent readers.

REFLECTIVE QUESTIONS

1. Attention and memory are identified as skills students need to become readers. Describe some brain-compatible classroom activities to strengthen attending and memory recall abilities.

2. If you are reading this book as part of a study group, as a group, make a list of strategies teachers can use to focus and direct their students' attention to learning tasks.

3. Declarative memory has two parts: semantic and episodic. How are they different?

4. Give some examples of episodic memory skills for developing readers that can be supported through classroom activities. Explain how semantic memory skills would be supported through different activities.

5. When teachers understand the energy requirements that reading places on emergent readers, they can structure classroom activities with children's needs in mind. Give an example of a reading task, what is requested of the students, how much time the activity will take, and what appropriate student responses would be.

Breaking the Reading Code

6

T he road to building a reading brain for decoding words and achieving reading fluency is not a uniform, one-size-fits-all path. Every teacher knows that children in each kindergarten and first-grade classroom exhibit a wide range of reading potential. Some children have already developed skills that put them in good stead to learn. They are motivated, attentive, can concentrate, and are relatively well organized. Many, but not all, of these children are on their way to becoming competent readers by the end of first grade. In the real-life classroom, teachers must be prepared to meet the needs of all children regardless of their level of preparedness.

> *The road to building a reading brain for decoding words and achieving reading fluency is not a uniform, one-size-fits-all path.*

READING AND LANGUAGE ARTS GUIDELINES FOR KINDERGARTEN AND FIRST GRADE

Because education in the United States is decentralized, each state's department of education sets forth educational guidelines and curricula. A review of reading and language arts standards across the nation reveals a consistent focus on reading and literacy during the primary years. A summary of generally accepted skills for mastery in kindergarten and first grade includes:

Word analysis with phonemic awareness, phonological processing, and skills for decoding

Fluency or speed of processing through skills ranging from identifying letter names to producing letter sounds to reading controlled text

Systematic vocabulary development, including learning specific words and word-recognition strategies

Reading comprehension, including the ability to predict what will happen, compare information from different sources, and answer essential questions, such as who, what, why, and what if

Literary response and analysis that progresses from character focus, setting, and recognizing important events in kindergarten to plot and story design in the first grade

Writing strategies and applications, beginning with upper- and lowercase letters and knowledge of letter sounds in kindergarten and moving to word and sentence production during first grade

Curriculum plans and frameworks for reading skills include specific student objectives and frequently provide examples of expected student responses. With regard to decoding and word recognition, for example, a child may be expected to blend sounds to be able to read one-syllable decodable words during the kindergarten year. For comparison, a first grader may be expected to use knowledge of vowel digraphs and r-controlled letter-sound associations to read words. In this case, a vowel digraph /ea/ would be recognized for its variance in "bear" and "seat." The expectations are clear. The public education system expects kindergarten students to work with individual sounds. First-grade students are expected to develop an awareness of words and their relationship to speech and conventions of print and to expand their reading word base.

STRUCTURING THE BRAIN FOR DECODING

The brain is hardwired for speech, not reading. As we discussed in Chapter 2, the initial pathway for oral language begins when a sound is perceived. The pathway for reading, however, begins with visual input. To read, the brain must interpret signals that are received from the visual cortex and co-opt parts of an existing system for listening and speaking to create a new pathway that processes print for meaning. Building a reading brain does not happen with naturally designated neural mechanisms for reading; the reading system must be developed.

> *Building a reading brain does not happen with naturally designated neural mechanisms for reading; the reading system must be developed.*

Structured teaching of phonological processes systematically leads the emerging reader's brain to facilitate links between the areas of the brain that need to be connected for reading. This allows words stored in implicit long-term memory for speaking or listening to be reconsidered and manipulated when they appear as print symbols. Children become aware of phonemes by working with sounds they already know. They blend sounds, segment words into sounds, replace sounds, add sounds, and delete sounds through structured phonemic play. Each time sounds and combinations of sounds are introduced in another way, the child is engaged with brain work through practice and co-articulation. The automatic process for phoneme manipulation can then become a part of long-term memory as an initial skill fundamental to the entire reading process. With practice, children come to associate visual patterns with words that they hear and speak.

Mastering Decoding With Phonological Processes

We use phonological processes as an umbrella term to identify children's conscious mental operations, perception, interpretation, recall, and production around the sound structure of oral language when they learn to decode successfully (Moats, 2001; Torgesen, Wagner, & Rashotte, 1994). Phonological processing requires a child to be able to segment and blend phonemes, pronounce words, identify words and syllables, detect syllable stress, and remember names and lists (Moats, 2001). It turns out that neither the ability to hear the difference between two phonemes nor the ability to produce them is as important to effective decoding as an awareness that individual sounds exist, can be manipulated, and be stored in long-term memory for ordered recall (Adams, 1990). A child needs many concepts and skills in order to become comfortable with the abstractions and manipulations for successful decoding of text. This section describes print awareness and alphabetic principle through phonics, while vocabulary development, processing speed, spelling, and writing are addressed later as skills that develop in tandem with the decoding processes.

Phonemic Awareness

Phonemic awareness is a conscious understanding that words are made of individual sounds (phonemes) from speech, and the ultimate awareness that these sounds represent letters of the alphabet. As we gain new insight into the reading brain and the reading process, it appears that most children need focused teaching to be skilled in phonemic awareness. Many reading experts identify a lack of phonemic awareness as a major cause of reading difficulties in children and adults who are poor readers (Adams, Foorman, Lundberg, &

Beeler, 1998a; Liberman, Shankweiler, & Liberman, 1999; Lyon & Fletcher, 2001). For adults who already know how to read, it seems quite logical that sounds heard in speech are paired with the letters on the printed page. However, Marilyn Jager Adams and her colleagues identify ". . . that without direct instructional support, phonemic awareness eludes roughly 25 percent of middle-class first graders and substantially more of those who come from less literacy-rich backgrounds" (Adams et al., 1998a, p. 19). To address the serious reading problems children have when they cannot hear, identify, or understand the concept of phonemes, these professors have developed a classroom curriculum specifically for phonemic awareness. (See the Instructional Resources.)

Phonemic awareness can be taught through planned activities for rhyming, alliteration, oddity tasks, phoneme segmentation, phoneme blending, phoneme manipulation, and syllable splitting. Activities designed to develop specific skills for reading may appear to be child's play. However, this work is not the same as the random, spontaneous activities that children engaged in during their infancy and preschool years to develop oral language.

In Chapter 4, we discussed developing phonemic awareness through rhyming and oddity activities that are addressed during the preschool years. Now we look at more advanced phonological processing skills of phoneme segmentation, phoneme blending, phoneme manipulation, and syllable splitting.

Phoneme segmentation requires children to break words into the smallest possible sounds they can distinguish. In the case of "hand," this would be "h-a-n-d" with children providing sounds for each letter rather than identifying letter names. The opposite of phonemic segmentation is phoneme blending. To blend, the teacher pronounces sounds with an exaggerated, slow pronunciation "h—a—n—d," then asks children to put the sounds together and to say them quickly as a meaningful word.

In phoneme manipulation, children are asked to change the sound they hear at the beginning or end of a word to another sound and, consequently, to another word. Note that the results may be a real or nonsense word. For example, children are given the word "fox" and the teacher asks that the beginning sound be changed to the /b/ sound. The response is "box." If children are asked to change the middle sound to /a/, they generally laugh as they realize that "bax" is not a real word. Phoneme manipulation places

> *Phoneme manipulation places extended demands on oral language structures as this sensory input is for deciphering individual sounds from words that are familiar in their entirety.*

extended demands on oral language structures as this sensory input is for deciphering individual sounds from words that are familiar in their entirety.

When children are asked to engage in phoneme syllable splitting, the teacher gives a word such as "dog" and the children are asked to give the beginning sound in isolation. When asked for the beginning sound, they would respond "d-d-d-d." Or, if asked to give the rest of the word without the beginning sound, they would say "og." For these tasks of phonemic awareness, the brain begins to reshape pathways that are a part of the oral language process. The neural pathways children use for reading begin with those used for oral language interpretation. These are then co-opted to connect and to make sense out of sound and letter relationships.

> *For these tasks of phonemic awareness, the brain begins to reshape pathways that are a part of the oral language process.*

Print Awareness

Awareness that print represents sounds and words provides a foundation for the child's brain that is under construction for reading. Although this awareness happens gradually, it is a monumental building block in the reading process. Print awareness develops in most children through interaction with their environment prior to school attendance. Experiences with pictures, colors, shapes, and symbols bring the concepts of print to the brain's attention. Children may recognize the logo for McDonald's or Kmart or the title of a Dr. Seuss book. Gradually, they begin to recognize a word such as "zoo" for its unique appearance. Susan Hall and Louisa Moats (1999) refer to this type of pre-alphabetic learning as *logographic reading.* Letter recognition, phoneme processing and maneuvering, learning sounds with attached letters or letter strings, and predicting relationships between letters and sounds are all dependent on the abstract concept that sounds and words are represented by patterns of written symbols.

Reading depends on an awareness of how alphabetic letters are represented through their phonological structure as words. During the transitional phase of putting letters to sounds, children must recognize that phonemes may overlap or run together in speech, but the phonemes as letters are represented distinctly in print. For example, "next door" becomes co-articulated in speech and sounds to a child like "nex store" or "an animal" may appear to be "an nanimal." Production of individual sounds in words, such as strings of consonants, consonant blends, or vowels, can be vocalized at a rate of about 8 to 10 per second. Because speaking sounds occurs so rapidly, Liberman et al. (1999) maintain it may be difficult for some children to determine how a spoken word or letter string is spelled. As children become more familiar with phonemes, their sounds, and their letter representations, they become adept at automatically reconciling these inconsistencies between sounds and the letters that represent them.

Alphabetic Principle Through Phonics

Phonics is a system to identify symbols used in alphabetic writing that represent sounds. Phonics is used by Moats (2001) to describe sound-symbol reading instruction, which may also be referred to as a phonics approach to teaching reading (p. 234). Almost all beginning reading programs include phonics instruction, but there are many different approaches among the existing programs. The National Institute for Literacy's document *Put Reading First: The Research Building Blocks for Teaching Children to Read* (Center for the Improvement of Early Reading Achievement, 2001) identifies six distinct methods for phonics instruction:

> Synthetic phonics converts letters or combinations of letters into sounds, then blends sounds for recognizable words.
>
> Analytic phonics scrutinizes the letter-sound relationships in words that are already known, but does not pronounce isolated sounds. Analogy-based phonics identifies unknown words by word families.
>
> Phonics through spelling segments words into phonemes, then develops new words using the phonemes that have been learned.
>
> Embedded phonics exposes children to phonics as examples become available through text.
>
> Onset-rime phonics identifies sounds before the first vowel (the onset), then addresses the remainder of the word (the rime) (adapted from Center for the Improvement of Early Reading Achievement, 2001, p. 13).

Children learn that letters represent the sounds of spoken language and not that the letters of the alphabet each have a sound. Consider the elusive /k/ sound, which is represented by the words "cup, kettle, deck, school, and oblique." Children can easily learn the sound and then anchor the sound to a letter or letter sequence (a grapheme). In addition to mimicking the way alphabetic writing was invented, this sequence gives the brain a logical way for ordering and storing the sounds and their accompanying letters for retrieval.

> *Children learn that letters represent the sounds of spoken language and not that the letters of the alphabet each have a sound.*

An effective phonics program has instructional components that

- give teachers support for systematic instruction
- build understanding for students about relationships between sounds and letters, and provide practice for what is learned with words, sentences, text, and writing

- are modifiable based on student assessment
- include related learning for alphabetic knowledge, phonemic awareness, vocabulary development, and text reading (Center for the Improvement of Early Reading Achievement, 2001)

Data from the National Institute of Child Health and Human Development do not support any particular approach to teaching phonics (Fletcher & Lyon, 1998). Likewise, there is no specific sequence for sound introduction, or number of sounds, or set of rules that identify the ideal phonics program. We strongly emphasize that, to read, children must understand the sound-letter relationships that are studied through the teaching of systematic phonics. However, programs using a variety of phonics techniques have been successful for students. Phonics programs that teachers use often combine several approaches. A sound-to-symbol relationship fits the needs of first-grade children at this stage of reading development.

Brain-Compatible Phonics Instruction

First, let us be clear. Phonics instruction cannot stand alone as a reading program. Children need simultaneous instruction to develop vocabulary; build understanding and comprehension; acquire listening skills; express ideas through spoken language; practice letter, word, and sentence writing; and develop a repertoire of words that can be spelled correctly (Center for the Improvement of Early Reading Achievement, 2001; Fletcher & Lyon,

> *Phonics instruction cannot stand alone as a reading program.*

1998). Phonics instruction is just one element of a complete building plan for reading. Let's look at some guidelines for brain-compatible phonics instruction.

Sounds to Letters, Not Letters to Sounds. Programs that introduce the 26 letters of the alphabet and then attach sounds to the letters not only appear to be ineffective, but they can cause confusion for students (Liberman et al., 1999; Moats, 1998). A teaching program that presents print-to-sound teaches only part of the code. This approach, which is found in some conventional phonics programs, leaves gaps for sounds that are represented. Twelve of the approximately 40 phonemes remain unexpressed when phonics is taught according to the 26 letters of the alphabet.

Furthermore, in a letter-to-sound approach, some letters have no uniquely defined job. For example, the letter /c/ shares sounds with /k/ and /s/. Some letter names bear little relationship to the sounds of the letter they represent. For example, the letter /x/ is named "eks" and sounds like /ks/ or /z/. Children may confuse these sounds during spelling and attempt to spell a word, such as "box," as "boks" or "boz." Reading expert Louisa Moats (1998) encourages explicit teaching to distinguish each sound and then to attach a letter or letters to the sound. Children may be asked to identify the sounds in words such as "mat," "sad," "pan," "pale," or "made." If children know the rules that govern short and long vowels, they can apply the rules to these predictable words.

Primary Word Walls. Word walls used in some primary classrooms can be effective when they are designed to reinforce vocabulary development. Word walls for phonics, however, can be illogical, complex, and confusing if they are based solely on the alphabet. An illogical word wall list for /Aa/ might include "and, away, all, are." A first-grade child who tries to make decoding sense out of this list containing irregular sounds for the letter /a/ may become confused about letters and sound relationships.

Orthographic Rules. Almost all words are completely regular by orthographic rule, but words use patterns that are somewhat obscure and do not exist peacefully with other decoding rules. An example would be a rule that states all words ending with a /v/ must have an /e/ at the end. The words "shove," "live," and "leave" all have the required /e/ after the /v/. But the final /e/ rule that says the preceding vowel should make a long sound is in conflict. Teachers identify these inconsistencies through a systematic and explicit approach

> *Much of the predictability of English comes not from individual letters, but from letter spelling units where two or more letters together make a sound.*

to teaching phonics with orthographic rules. Children, then, can make sense out of letters, sounds, and words and develop the capacity to deal with the inconsistencies of English.

Identification of Common Letter Blends and Word Families. Children may be confused when they are asked to use a word attack strategy that sounds out words letter by letter. Much of the predictability of English comes not from individual letters, but from letter spelling units where two or more letters together make a sound. A better approach, one firmly based on phonics instruction, is to identify the following when approaching the traditional "sounding out" process for unknown words:

common consonant blends (e.g., /bl/, /br/, /pr/, /shr/, /thr/, /tw/)

vowel graphemes (e.g., /ai/, /eigh/, /ie/, /ough/, /ou/, /augh/)

word families (e.g., a base word, such as care, identified in careful, caring, and uncaring)

A letter-to-sound strategy, primary word walls based on the alphabet, incomplete orthographic rules, or sounding out individual letters in words are merely some of the teaching practices that can lead to confusion for a child's brain that seeks order and patterns that are meaningful. Teachers who understand the child's brain as a pattern-seeking organ are more likely to provide clear, logical word recognition strategies for children to use.

WORD RECOGNITION GAINS SOPHISTICATION

As children move through the primary grades, they gain more sophisticated ways of learning new words. They progress, for example, from sounding out all of the letters to recognizing letter patterns and phonemes, then to decoding words by syllables and identifying morphological components. Using the word "uncomfortable," first-grade instruction would sound out the phonemes, u/n/c/o/m/f/or/t/a/b/le. Second-grade students would look at syllables, un/com/fort/a/ble. This allows them to extend letter combinations, seek larger orthographic units, and look for predictable beginnings and endings. By the third grade, students' advanced abilities allow them to look at larger and more complex orthographic units. Third graders would approach this sample word as un/comfort/able.

Instruction can follow a progression of word recognition strategies during the early elementary years that builds to the use of meaningful units of morphemes, words, word origins, and understanding through a core knowledge base in the fourth grade and beyond (Moats, Furry, & Brownell, 1998).

Brain-Compatible Teaching
Programs for Phonological Processing

Effective teachers respond to children's word attack needs with classroom strategies that are designed to captivate young readers. One such response is a phonics and spelling supplement developed by Cunningham, Hall, and Heggie (1994). During a 15-minute whole-class teaching block, children work with an individual pocket chart and letters. The children initially develop two-letter words and progress to making bigger and bigger words. Discovering a mystery word is the climax of each lesson. Children are delighted with the suspense that the mystery word creates, particularly as words become more complex. Each child's brain is primed during this group lesson with neural hooks to build connections and categories for sound-letter correspondences and word families.

Another supplemental program gives repeated exposure to spoken language during beginning reading phonological processing. By using oral language exposure, Goldsworthy's *Sourcebook of Phonological Awareness Activities:*

Children's Classic Literature (1998) encourages children to form phonics bins, which are clusterings of sounds that have properties in common, such as /a/ in cat, sat, and bat, or the beginning sound of /b/ in bear, box, or balloon. Children can use these theoretical bins to accumulate sound categories that they recognize as speech sounds. Exposures to phonological processing, representation, and deviations, as Goldsworthy refers to them, strengthen the sound categories that children develop. Activities in this program include classic stories that provide complex, but naturally familiar words. Stories are read and discussed at least three times. The stories may be accompanied by a flannel board presentation, hand puppets, or role-play. Parents support the process at home by reading and talking about the stories and particularly discussing the vocabulary. In this way, the vocabulary becomes familiar to the children before activities require work with phonological processes.

Using "Goldilocks and the Three Bears" as a target story, activities may include simple word-counting procedures, such as, "How many words do you hear in 'The bears went for a walk'?" More complex activities ask students to change the first two sounds in a pair of words. In this case, "middle sized" becomes "siddle mized," and "big voice" becomes "vig boice." Children enjoy the novelty of this kind of activity. The author emphasizes that activities move from sounds to letters, which, as we have seen, leads to logical, confusion-free phonological development for children (Goldsworthy, 1998).

To summarize, students achieve intended outcomes for phonological processing when they are motivated to read and when they are exposed to a logical sequence of instruction. The National Institute of Child Health and Human Development (NICHD) reported on studies that were conducted at 36 different sites to check reading development. The studies included 34,501 children with normal reading development and children whose reading development was impaired. Interventions that produced successful readers went beyond explicit teaching of phonics. Successful readers were encouraged to read and write for enjoyment and were stimulated to do so with practices, such as those described in the two previous examples, that fostered positive attitudes toward reading (Fletcher & Lyon, 1998).

READING BEYOND DECODING

Reading is a developmental process that involves being able to identify words in text, understand what the words mean, seek connections for word meanings, and do all this with speed and fluency. In kindergarten and first grade, reading instruction moves beyond phonological processing skills that are needed for decoding to include comprehension skills, speed of processing (fluency), and development of sight vocabulary.

Building Vocabulary for Comprehending Text

Comprehension depends greatly on the words a child knows and can call on automatically. Educators are encouraged to provide a wide variety of listening and print exposure experiences during the first 2 years of school, including books based on the alphabet, informational stories, classic and contemporary literature, children's magazines and newspapers, dictionaries, and reference materials. Teachers need to initiate questioning and discussion before, during, and after reading these materials in order to help students comprehend and draw meaning from them as well as new vocabulary.

It is surprising to realize that children attending preschools are not given a learning advantage for vocabulary development when the curriculum emphasizes early decoding and pre-alphabetic skills at the expense of language development activities (Biemiller, 2003a). Consider also that some kindergarten teachers spend as much as 40 percent of their language arts instructional time on sound-letter instruction and decoding unfamiliar words that children have not previously seen and cannot define (Bucuvalas & Juel, 2002). Emphasis on vocabulary building must happen concurrently with phonological processing and decoding instruction during the early school years.

Vocabulary development initially occurs through talking. Teachers who discuss the meaning of words with children and provide opportunities for children to engage in conversations about words enhance their spoken language and expand the ways children store language and vocabulary in the brain for retrieval. For example, share time in kindergarten and first grade helps children learn how to express their ideas or experiences in complete, coherent, syntactically correct sentences.

When a teacher also provides opportunities for students to respond to the vocabulary used by their peers, the experience takes on an additional level of learning sophistication (Beck, McKeown, & Kucan, 2003). A teacher may ask another student, "What does it mean when Sheri said that she was confused by the picture?" Or, "What did Manuel say to make us understand that he was embarrassed?" Providing many experiences for oral language comprehension makes sense, because how well children are able to comprehend during listening appears to be an excellent predictor for future success with reading comprehension (Aaron, 1995). Comprehension, the ultimate goal of reading, coupled with vocabulary development, will be covered in depth in Chapter 8.

Processing Written Symbols, Orthography

Orthography is the visual pattern for written language with features of graphemes, phonology, and semantics. At what speed does the brain process the orthography of print? Children develop processing speed as they learn more words at an automatic level. When kindergarten and first-grade children develop a repository of words stored in long-term memory and decode at an automatic level, they are able to move rapidly along each written line, seeing each letter and each word, but being detained by none.

Many areas of the brain are involved with the reading of even an individual word, and if words are not known by the child at an automatic level, the process can stall at any juncture. If the child is not able to process words rapidly and automatically, comprehension suffers. Reading with fluency begins to develop in the early years, but it may take several years before these skills are comfortably in place. Chapter 9 will discuss fluency in more depth.

> *When kindergarten and first-grade children develop a repository of words stored in long-term memory and decode at an automatic level, they are able to move rapidly along each written line, seeing each letter and each word, but being detained by none.*

Teaching Sight Words

Teaching sight words is not an either/or proposition. An emergent reader who is building strong decoding skills can simultaneously learn and will automatically add common sight words to an ever-expanding sight vocabulary. Words that are known by sight are taught using rote memory techniques or through frequent exposure. Once learned at the automatic recall level, the words are stored in long-term memory within neural networks of similar words and experiences. Words such as "and," "from," "the," "of," "to," "that," "for," "was," "are," "with," and "you" should be recognized by sight, as they are often not included with sound-to-print instruction that prepares students to read decodable text. In addition, as children learn sight words, more interesting stories are accessible for children to read.

There are limitations to teaching sight vocabulary. Some children with excellent memory skills learn to easily store new words in long-term memory, rather than going through the hard work of learning the orthographic rules for decoding. Remedial work with students who are identified as unsuccessful decoders indicates that some of these children have excellent memory skills for sight words. They may be generally successful readers until the middle or end of

> *Remedial work with students who are identified as unsuccessful decoders indicates that some of these children have excellent memory skills for sight words.*

second grade, as long as they read relatively short words. However, when they are faced with text that has longer multisyllable words, words that look similar, and words with many deviations for letter sequence, they begin to show signs of reading difficulties. Instruction that encourages students to learn too many sight words during the early years can give readers a false sense of reading success, when actually they are taxing memory capabilities in place of developing decoding strategies.

Teaching Spelling and Writing With Decoding

Learning to spell should occur simultaneously with learning to assign letters to sounds for decoding (Adams et al., 1998a; Fletcher & Lyon, 1998; Liberman et al., 1999). This allows children to learn the same new patterns of language across the domains of listening, reading, writing, and spelling, thus strengthening the networks of neural connections formed in the brain as it categorizes words first for how they look and sound, then for how they are represented by letters, and, finally, for their meaning. Words are learned with efficiency and with greater likelihood for retention and retrieval when they are practiced at different times in different ways through phonological processing instruction that is paired with spelling and writing.

> *Learning to spell should occur simultaneously with learning to assign letters to sounds for decoding (Adams et al., 1998a; Fletcher & Lyon, 1998; Liberman et al., 1999).*

Spelling

Spelling instruction can be based on a number of premises, such as sound-symbol correspondences, syllable patterns, orthographic rules, word meanings, word derivation, or word origin. We know, however, instruction is most compatible with the reading brain when spelling words are meaningfully organized into groups with common word patterns and coherently sequenced grade by grade. Moats (2001, p. 153) suggests a spelling program linked to phoneme awareness in kindergarten, consonant and vowel correspondence for first grade, more complex spelling patterns for second grade, and syllabication, compounds, and word endings for third grade.

A spelling list of 10 to 12 words per week may contain words children are using in their reading or writing that exemplify orthographic patterns from a sequenced word study program. Teachers frequently include additional words that students find confusing and that need to be clarified. Ideally, the study of orthography, the spelling of words, in the early school years is closely matched with words that occur in reading texts with high frequency, but spelling lists also contain some commonly misspelled words in the mix.

Systematic instruction for phoneme-to-grapheme spelling is emphasized through the second grade and beyond. As children become more sophisticated with their ability to decipher new words, selection of words for spelling study takes a vocabulary-building emphasis. Intense spelling instruction for letter and word patterns in the early school years secures an understanding of words and their parts that allows older children to employ self-initiated analysis techniques with new vocabulary they encounter as they read.

Story-Telling and Writing

Children in kindergarten and first grade are capable of developing complex thoughts far in advance of their ability to express these thoughts in writing. When they are expected to write independently, the difference between what they know about words and what they are physically capable of recording on paper becomes apparent. Recognizing this disparity, teachers can take an active role during their students' early writing efforts by allowing students to dictate their ideas and stories. This intensive one-to-one interaction can be handled by parent volunteers or older student helpers who write them down for the children, or the whole class can become involved in story development as the teacher writes on an overhead projector or large chart. Writing, as a developmental skill, is a natural companion to the process of learning to read.

Although writing is a natural partner to a reading program, it does not happen easily. Writing places a new set of demands on the developing brain by calling on the motor cortex to respond in new ways. Picture a child who is beginning to experiment with writing. The youngster concentrates on holding a pencil between the thumb, pointer finger, and middle finger. At first, this feels and looks awkward, and the child must concentrate on gripping the pencil with the appropriate amount of tension and really think about touching the lead of the pencil to the paper. As the fingers press and move the pencil, the child consciously thinks about the shapes that are being made, staying within the lines, and manipulating the pencil.

While this struggle is visible, what is going on in the brain is not. Planning, timing, and execution of finger, hand, and arm movements, initiated in the premotor and motor cortex, are ultimately orchestrated by the frontal lobes. The cerebellum, located at the lower back of the brain, unconsciously coordinates the precise hand movements when a child puts marks on the paper (Berninger & Richards, 2002).

With practice, the neural circuits used for writing eventually function automatically and the child no longer needs to be conscious of this very complex process. Teachers can provide other classroom activities, often thought of as art or craft projects such as stenciling, tracing, coloring within small spaces, cutting, and pasting, that act as developmental activities for the mechanics of writing. In a well-designed program, writing and spelling work in tandem with reading, so that children have an outlet to expand complex thinking skills and express complex thoughts and ideas.

Children progress from being ready to read to decoding and from developing vocabulary and understanding to the ability to read with fluency and accuracy. In tandem, they begin to learn spelling patterns and start to record their own ideas in writing. Not all children develop these skills at the same rate. The next chapter addresses important considerations to catch children before they are unsuccessful with any aspect of their reading development.

REFLECTIVE QUESTIONS

1. The brain has structures that are hardwired to attend to and produce speech. What is different about the demands that are placed on the brain to respond to input for reading?

2. If you are reading this book as part of a study group, ask three people to prepare a short lesson that plays with sounds for phoneme awareness. Have the group define concepts children are learning when they practice sounds through these exercises.

3. Prepare an outline or concept map for a short faculty presentation to review the five types of phonics instruction discussed in this chapter. Consider a discussion about how phonics is taught at your school.

4. Writing is a natural accompaniment to a reading program. In what ways do teachers prime their students and their brains for the physical process of writing?

5. Comment on some of the advantages and disadvantages of teaching sight words.

Assessing and Responding to At-Risk Readers

7

THE CASE FOR EARLY ASSESSMENT

Teachers find that some children enter school already reading, some are ready to read, and others lack even basic print awareness. The National Association for the Education of Young Children states, ". . . most children learn to read at age six or seven, a few learn at four, some learn at five, and others need intensive individualized support to learn to read at eight or nine" (NAEYC, 1998, p. 30). This means that, as early as kindergarten, there may be a 2-year variation in reading ability in a single classroom that expands by third grade. A range of potential abilities, coupled with differences in background experiences, interests, personality, and temperament, challenges teachers who are expected to produce academic results for every child in a predetermined time frame based on grade-level standards (NAEYC, 1998). With a large variation in language abilities even among 5- and 6-year-olds, teachers find they must identify children who are at risk for academic failure early in the first year of school.

This chapter approaches formal reading instruction with the belief that all children are ready for reading instruction when they enter school, and then discusses assessments for successful and struggling emergent readers. Specific programs will be identified to meet the varying needs of children who are at risk of reading failure and for those who stumble along the way. Children who enter school with good oral language skills in English and are ready to read but subsequently fail to make adequate progress must be identified. Likewise, those who have insufficient oral language development need assessment, for neither group of children learns to read at expected levels without instructional interventions (Lyon & Fletcher, 2001).

No Waiting Allowed

Neuroscientists using positron emission tomography (PET) scans have identified critical developments in the brain between the ages of 4 and 12. During this time, learning appears to surge. Imaging technology follows the brain's consumption of glucose, the fuel nerve cells use when they are active and make new connection among themselves. Prize-winning science writer Ronald Kotulak (1997) describes this energy spurt as a time "... when the brain seemed to glow like a nuclear reactor, pulsating at levels 225 percent higher than adult brains" (p. 36). Kotulak speculates that this is a time that the brain determines to keep or prune connections as it eagerly seeks stimuli from the senses.

> *In terms of cognition, during the primary years children are extremely responsive to instruction with brains that are more malleable, plastic, and open to new learning than at any other time during their formal education.*

The years from birth through age 8 are furthermore considered to be critical for literacy development. In terms of cognition, during the primary years children are extremely responsive to instruction with brains that are more malleable, plastic, and open to new learning than at any other time during their formal education.

Educators' responsibility to every child, particularly during this period of rapid brain development, is to make learning accessible and challenging for every student and to provide appropriate interventions for those who do not keep up. All children must have their learning needs met, even if the necessary intervention programs are time and personnel intensive and more costly for children who are not progressing as expected.

Educators know that while children arrive at school with a wide range of backgrounds for reading, they all are expected to meet state and federal performance standards. The obstacles to be overcome by both teachers and students sometimes look formidable. Consider a study conducted by Susan B. Neuman, Assistant Secretary for Elementary and Secondary Education, U.S. Department of Education, and her colleagues (2001). The study took place in four neighborhoods of Philadelphia that represented two middle-class and two low-income areas. In each instance, the researchers determined how many children were in the area, how many places were available to purchase children's books, and the number of different book titles that were available within the geographic area. Additionally, logographic signs were identified and childcare center libraries were scrutinized. The researchers found that in the best situation the neighborhood potential for books to be purchased provided approximately 12 book titles for each child. Researchers deemed this number as a significant choice of books. In the neighborhood with the least print availability, there were 33 book titles in total—all of which were coloring books—available for approximately 1,000 children.

The researchers identify three educational ramifications from this study that focused on book availability in neighborhoods. First, they refer to the "Mathew effects" in which children with more opportunity for book exposure grow in academic achievement, while those with less print availability become weaker in their ability to break the code for reading text. An environmental opportunity hypothesis identified earlier by Keith Stanovich (1986) speaks to the fact that children who have limited exposure to print are less likely to be able to hear the phonology associated with print, something we know is essential for learning to read. Second, Neuman et al. refer to a familiarity hypothesis: children who are familiar with books and stories develop mental models that go with reading different kinds of text. With familiarity comes comfort with reading. The third hypothesis the researchers identify is the most powerful—the knowledge gap. Individuals learn, really learn with a depth of understanding, what they are able to access through print. The good news reported by Neuman is that something can be done about the knowledge gap. Teachers can provide carefully constructed educational environments that are rich with exposure not only to direct instruction, but also to large numbers of books to captivate young minds.

Important studies such as this one help educators to understand the differences that potentially could be represented among schoolchildren from different socioeconomic groups. Realize, also, that information reported in this study represents *only* the environmental impact upon children from English-speaking families. Teachers are faced with another set of considerations when children learn English as a second language.

ENGLISH LANGUAGE LEARNERS

In an ideal educational environment, students whose first language is not English are assessed for English language skills immediately on entering the school system. In the 1999–2000 school year, an estimated 9.3 percent, or 4.4 million, American students were English language learners (ELLs). Of these, 77 percent were native Spanish speakers (Antunez, 2002). Each student who is not proficient in English needs a reading program that is tailored to that student's specific needs. While assessments that determine the level of competence a student possesses in both English and the child's primary language are needed, some additional questions can add meaningful information to help the classroom teacher to make instructional decisions:

Does the primary language have a Roman alphabet? A written form?

Does it contain phonemes and how do the phonemes compare to English sounds?

Can the student fluently speak, read, and write the primary language?

How well does the student speak English?

How old is the student?

What staff, programs, and resources are available to teach this student? (Antunez, 2002)

The student's fluency in English, along with an assessment of available school resources, is used to determine the language of initial reading instruction. For students who are not proficient in English, answers to the previous questions prompt decisions about the type of program—primary language, English-only, or bilingual (integrated primary language and English)—that will be appropriate when these choices are available. Unfortunately, many districts and states do not offer a range of appropriate choices, and many students do not receive the support they need to succeed with written and spoken English.

Children who lack exposure to adequate oral language preparation in their native language, who live or have lived in an unsafe environment, lack a family that provides loving care, or who have had little formal schooling, are best served in a bilingual program (Linquanti, 1999). A bilingual program can help develop oral language for English language learners in both their native language and in English. Language development in one language tends to nurture development in the other when schools provide an environment that allows children to learn in both languages (Cummins, 2000).

Children who come into the formal education system already speaking and reading well in their native language are often placed in a regular classroom that provides an English-only program. The background information about language that they already possess provides a foundation for instruction in an English-only program. These programs are particularly successful when they have instruction provided in a varied format that actively engages students in speaking, reading, and writing.

Issues for English language learners are diverse. Although their needs for decoding are similar to those of their English-speaking peers, ELLs may need additional practice and modified instruction through the regular education program. One difficulty ELLs experience is that the sounds of English phonemes are often different from those in their native language. For example,

Spanish-speaking children are familiar with similar sounds for the consonants b, c, d, f, l, m, n, p, q, s, and t in their primary language. However, the vowels are named differently. There are challenges to teaching decoding skills, phonemic awareness, and phonics to ELLs. However, teachers can effectively teach skills necessary for reading competence if they have knowledge about their students and about their native language (Antunez, 2002). Teachers who lack background in the primary language of their students frequently benefit from receiving expert consultation from another educator. Realistically, with the many languages children bring, this is often not possible.

> *Although their needs for decoding are similar to those of their English-speaking peers, ELLs may need additional practice and modified instruction through the regular education program.*

Often school districts have an inadequate number of appropriate assessment instruments and trained personnel to determine if a child has English language acquisition needs, and if those needs occur in tandem with a learning disability. Special education programs in certain districts often show an over-representation of English language learners. To counteract overrepresentation of non-English speakers who receive special education services, schools are urged to identify children with limited or no English ability early and to create school environments with instructional strategies that have proven to be successful for these at-risk students (Ortiz, 2001).

We have provided two particular instances where environmental issues block student success with reading—low socioeconomic status and lack of exposure to English. We also know that biological or neurological differences among children are also a cause of disparities in reading achievement. Understanding the need for assessment, having a plan for reading instruction that targets most children, and providing intervention for those students with special needs are appropriate expectations for our public school systems. First, we will look at reading assessment information and instructional responses for normally progressing readers, followed by assessments and intervention programs for students who need special consideration.

ASSESSMENT OF STUDENTS WITH REGULARLY DEVELOPING READING SKILLS

Children who progress normally in reading are for the most part assessed in the classroom through basal readers. The range of assessments that teachers use during the first 2 years of reading instruction covers concepts of print, phonemic awareness, phonics, fluency, oral reading, spelling, vocabulary, and comprehension. As students progress through the grades, teachers also assess students' ability related to organizational features of text and reference skills. Teachers use district or state guidelines to direct their assessment practices. Ongoing classroom assessment allows teachers to identify children who are not progressing in any skill area. Often additional instruction time or skills practice will remediate the problem through ongoing regular classroom interventions.

Instructional Responses to Assessment

Teachers frequently use strategies of pre-teach, re-teach, modify, model, and adjust as they respond to the diverse needs of their students. While there are many skill development designs that involve whole class instruction, teachers also find it helpful to use flexible classroom grouping to meet the needs of their varied student population. Usually, teachers decide to assess and reconfigure their instructional groups many times, even during the kindergarten year. When teachers find they need to work with small groups, it is important that children are able to work independently. Teachers often spend a considerable amount of time—5 weeks or more—at the beginning of the

> *Usually, teachers decide to assess and reconfigure their instructional groups many times, even during the kindergarten year.*

year to set up classroom procedures for students to work independently. As the rest of the class works at their desks or on projects at learning stations, the teacher is free to target instruction to meet the varying needs of children in a small group setting.

DIFFERENCES IN BRAIN DEVELOPMENT

The brains of children who cannot read easily may be working very hard, perhaps harder than the brains of those who have no difficulty. Neuroscientists have observed huge demands in the brain for glucose (energy), as poor readers struggle with reading tasks. But the students' hard work does not yield successful reading results. As you may recall from information discussed in Chapter 2, there may be a lack of connectedness in

> *Neuroscientists have observed huge demands in the brain for glucose (energy), as poor readers struggle with reading tasks.*

the reading system in some children's brains (Shaywitz, 2003). Good readers have integrated, smoothly functioning connections among the structures of a well-defined reading system. In contrast, dyslexic readers use ancillary connections and frequently do not connect to areas in the brain that effective readers use. These alternate connections may allow struggling readers to accurately read words, but do not permit them to attain and recall mental models for words that would allow fluent and automatic reading (Shaywitz & Shaywitz, 2001).

Digging Deeper Into Reading Disabilities

Dyslexia has been defined by Sally Shaywitz at Yale University as a cognitive deficit relating to phonological processing, particularly the ability to decode and recognize words and to write and spell. Based on her extensive research in the area of dyslexia, Shaywitz reports that brain-imaging studies revealed markedly different brain activation patterns in dyslexic readers compared to those in good readers (Shaywitz, 2003). While Shaywitz tends to identify all unsuccessful readers as dyslexic, other reading specialists use a variety of descriptions. Commonly used terminology includes "poor readers" (Moats, 2001), "children with special needs" (Vukelich, Christie, & Enz, 2002), "struggling readers" (Allington, 2001), or "disabled/impaired readers" (Fletcher & Lyon, 1998). Classroom teachers, too, would tell us that there is a range of struggling readers. Some children have minimal skill deficits while at the other end of the continuum are children who are identified with learning disabilities, and who qualify for special education services. There is not agreement among experts on a single term that adequately defines the variety of unsuccessful readers, nor the intensity of reading problems children experience. Based on the uniqueness of each child's brain, there is not a single instructional response to reading problems.

Regardless of terminology, many children who experience reading problems have been exposed to regular reading instruction and may exhibit abilities in higher-order reading skills of vocabulary, syntax, and reasoning discourse. Yet, they lack the ability to decode and read rapidly.

The inability to discern and manipulate abstractions associated with phonemes has been identified as a significant cause of many reading failures. A relatively small number of emergent readers, however, do not respond to regular or extended classroom interventions for phonemic awareness and decoding deficits. If these children are given additional instruction and practice, and they continue to fall further behind their classmates, they may have cognitive differences that block their ability to even think about phonemes.

In Chapter 5, we discussed the cognitive skills that need to be primed for the emerging reader. These skills, particularly attention, memory, concentration, and organization, may not be identified through traditional classroom testing. Traditional assessment determines what a child is able or unable to do.

However, traditional assessment does not provide information about how the brain is structured for reading when we look at students who are struggling with cognitive differences. P. G. Aaron, professor of education and school psychology at Indiana State University, suggests a "deeper elusive problem with cognitive processes that underlie reading" (Aaron, 1995, p. 345). An example of one such problem could be visual processing. In this instance, a child is unable to concentrate on or focus on tracking words or make the necessary conversions from the visual input to a sound or word output.

> *These skills, particularly attention, memory, concentration, and organization, may not be identified through traditional classroom testing.*

Much of the information we currently receive about aberrant brain function during attempts at reading come from studies that neuroscientists are conducting that compare brain imaging of successful and nonsuccessful readers using functional magnetic resonance imaging (fMRI) scanning technology. It is not possible, nor would we suggest, that a child having reading difficulties undergo a brain scan, but educators can increase the depth of their assessments and attempt more thorough observation methods. Differences in the struggling reader's brain that are related to how the brain processes during attempts at reading rather than what the child knows lead educators toward a different course for remediation.

One example of intense assessment and observation in reading intervention is the program developed at the Lindamood-Bell Clinic. Pat Lindamood and her colleagues at the clinic identify and treat individual reading deficiencies through sensory-cognitive function (Lindamood, Bell, & Lindamood, 1997). Assessments done by clinicians at the Lindamood Clinic use standard tests of reading progress and additionally check a child's ability to manipulate phonemes. The Lindamood program, different from and more intense than most interventions, uses a tactile/sensory approach. Children learn to pay attention to sounds by feeling what is happening with their mouths and to identify how they form sounds with labels such as "lip poppers" or "tongue tappers." This methodology progresses from oral sounds to having the child represent sounds with colored blocks. Ultimately, children progress to letters and words.

This sequence of instruction appears to activate the child's brain for attending to sounds through a tactile approach and stimulate a pathway to the brain's language centers for sound identification. It represents a cognitive response to reading difficulty that goes beyond traditional approaches for poor readers.

ASSESSMENT AND READING STANDARDS

Reading First legislation requires support at the state and local levels for the selection and implementation of informal and formal assessments beginning in kindergarten and first grade. These assessments identify progress of both normally progressing readers and children who are failing. An assessment committee funded by the federal government reviewed and applied stringent criteria to commercially available assessment tests. A report summarizing the work of the committee, prepared by Edward J. Kame'enui (2002), professor at the Institute for the Development of Educational Achievement (IDEA) and the College of Education at the University of Oregon, is available to educators. The committee identified 24 formal assessment measures that have sufficient evidence to be used for screening, diagnosis, progress monitoring, and measuring Reading First outcomes. Assessments that met the criteria for the five reading components of Reading First legislation (phonemic awareness, phonics, reading fluency, vocabulary development, and reading comprehension) are listed on the University of Oregon Web site. (See the Instructional Resources.) These assessments can be used for normally progressing children and for children whose reading is impaired.

Children with cognitive functioning deficiencies challenge educators to look more closely at the way these students interpret sensory input the brain receives for reading. When children experience serious reading difficulties, assessments administered by a psychologist or language specialist provide in-depth information about the prerequisite cognitive functions required for reading. Some examples of the many commercially available assessments include the Gray Oral Reading Test (Gort-3), the Phonological Awareness Test (PAT), and the Lindamood Auditory Conceptualization Test (LAC). Some assessments are directed toward one specific cognitive function, such as phonemic awareness; digit span; number, sentence, or word memory; short-term memory; auditory or verbal comprehension; or processing speed. Other assessments provide subtests for several of these cognitive functions. Combining assessment reports from a school psychologist or language speech pathologist with the teacher's classroom assessments and process observations provides a thorough picture of the struggling reader's strengths and needs. In this way, a complete battery of assessments can provide precise information to match deficit skills with an appropriate reading intervention program.

For educators, there is a strong message. The longer a child continues to struggle with an inefficient system for reading, the more urgent it becomes that we intervene. We observe this long-term effect, not by brain imaging, but by substantial research supported by the National Institute of Child Health and Human Development (NICHD). Without systematic, focused, and intensive intervention, the majority of children who enter school at risk for reading failure are rarely able to catch up with their peers who are nonimpaired readers (Lyon, 2003). It is our challenge and responsibility as educators to select reading intervention strategies and programs that will correct the weaknesses individual children experience in their language systems. Intensive reading programs appear to change the neural networks in a child's brain and activate the brain in different ways to create an effective pathway for word and sound recognition and ultimately for fluent reading.

READING INTERVENTION MODELS

Estimates of the number of children with serious reading problems in our schools today could be as high as 15 to 20 percent. This means that as many as 10 million children across the United States could be struggling with reading failure (Sherman, 2002). G. Reid Lyon (2003) paints an even more startling picture. He estimates the number of poor readers at 20 million. There is widespread agreement that an early assessment is needed for all children and that early-intervention programs can become preventative instruction for those who are identified as at risk for reading. Special education programs serve only 2.3 million students nationwide. This means that there could be as many as 17.7 million children who do not meet the criteria for special education services, but still need evidence-based early identification and prevention programs to succeed as fluent readers.

Reading intervention programs have specific goals. They are designed to target children who are making inadequate reading progress, provide flexible instruction to remediate deficit reading skills, and attain positive results. Elements of an effective reading program for prevention/intervention are defined by Joseph K. Torgesen (1998), a research professor of psychology and education at Florida State University: "Some of the word-level skills and knowledge these children will require instruction on include: phonemic awareness, letter-sound correspondences, blending skills, a small number of pronunciation conventions (i.e., silent e rule), use of context to help specify a word once it is partially or completely phonemically

> *Research, planning, and school staff commitment are essential to provide the type of intense remediation that accompanies a program designed for all children to achieve reading success.*

decoded, strategies for multisyllable words, and automatic recognition of high-frequency 'irregular' words." Furthermore, Torgesen emphasizes that this instruction should be embedded with meaningful reading and writing opportunities (p. 34). Research, planning, and school staff commitment are essential to provide the type of intense remediation that accompanies a program designed for all children to achieve reading success. We will discuss two models that have been selected for reading interventions, as they match the level of intensity required for student success.

A Tiered Approach

A model to successfully provide early identification of children who are at risk for reading problems and to promote success for students was designed by Professor Virginia Berninger and her colleagues from the University of Washington. A team of educators worked with 18 schools in the state of Washington in the late 1990s. The program, called the Student Responsive Delivery System, requires screening during its first tier. *Every* kindergarten through second-grade child is evaluated using research-based assessment measures that are brief, easy to administer, and accurately identify both reading and writing failure. Identified students receive Tier 1 instructional modifications and careful monitoring in the regular classroom. Teachers may pre-teach a lesson or re-teach a difficult concept as they pay careful attention to the needs of their at-risk students.

Tier 2 support is provided for children who do not make adequate progress even though they had Tier 1 special assistance. Teachers are prompted to identify children who do not make adequate progress in spite of the increased instructional attention. The intervention is intensified as a team of educators, usually consisting of teaching peers, scrutinizes classroom assessment data. At this stage, modifications are still provided at the regular classroom level. Rather than simple instructional modifications, the Tier 2 level provides intense interventions, which include supplementing the regular reading program with additional curriculum, changing how instruction is presented, using revised instructional materials, and providing extra skill practice.

If needed, Tier 3 moves beyond interventions within the general education classroom. The third level requires a multidisciplinary team to review all previous student assessment; add formal, standardized assessment; review student records; and possibly interview the student, teacher, and/or parents. An assessment and planning team at the third level most likely includes the school psychologist, a language speech specialist, reading teacher, special educator, and/or a general educator.

Students who have not been successful during the first two levels of intervention are generally in need of special education services. Responsible parties, including parents and educational support staff, come together to decide if the child meets special education criteria. If so, the child is identified as having a learning disorder that is affecting reading (Sherman, 2002). An Individualized Education Program (IEP) is developed with a written plan designed to address the child's individual reading needs. This plan identifies the child's strengths for reading as well as areas of deficit. Included with a child's IEP are global reading goals, benchmarks for progress, and specific objectives that will pave the way for grade-level appropriate reading development.

The three-tiered system of support designed by Berninger for needy readers is aligned with current practices for regular classroom interventions and for processes required to identify children for special education with two differences. First, the tiered plan identifies children early in their formal education, ideally before they experience failure and develop feelings of self-doubt. Second, the tiered approach is an expansion of student support or study teams that are in place at many schools. However, the three-tiered process contains steps that are more specific, defined, and intense than those we find at most schools.

Impressive results were realized from the model during the1998–1999 school year. The need for complete assessments in Tier 3 was cut by 73 percent from the previous program where children were assessed for special education without Tier 1 and Tier 2 interventions. Of the 215 students with reading problems who were identified for the study, 138 needed no further support following a year of intervention. Only 28 students needed special education services through Tier 3 intervention (Sherman, 2002).

An Early-Intervention Model

The Bethel School District in Oregon adopted an early-intervention program designed by University of Oregon's reading researchers, Dr. Edward Kame'enui and Deborah Simmons, to help children before they fell behind in reading. Before this early-intervention program, the Bethel School District reported that 15 percent of the students were unable to read when they left the first grade and subsequently 17 percent of the second graders were referred for special education in 1996–1997. End-of-the-year results after using the program found only 2 percent of the children leaving first grade as nonreaders.

Before adopting the new intervention program, an analysis of district reading programs revealed several practices that needed modification. Assessments for struggling readers were in place, but the information from the assessments was not used to influence classroom practices. Researchers found that while children were ready to begin preparation for reading at age 5, the district's kindergarten curriculum was socially, rather than academically, based. It was also determined that reading programs were not consistent from school to school across the district (Paglin, 2002).

The district adopted a preventative instructional model for all schools. Each kindergarten child was assessed during the second week of school for initial-sound and letter-naming fluency using Dynamic Indicators of Basic Early Literacy Skills (DIBELS), which includes a set of reading indicators and benchmarks for skill development. This tool reliably predicts later reading performance. Assessments took only 3 minutes to administer for each child. The assessment data, when combined with teacher observation, allowed students to be placed at *benchmark*—on track to meet district expectations and state standards, *strategic*—progressing, but behind expected levels, and *intensive*—at risk of failing to meet reading standards or goals. At the end of the first month of school, at-risk kindergarteners were already receiving an extra 30 minutes of reading instruction with a highly scripted program. During the year, the progress of kindergarten and first-grade students was carefully monitored and data-driven decisions were made based on students' instructional needs. End-of-the-year results reported positive reading advances for students. Teachers also reported that children were less likely to misbehave when they worked at an appropriate level for skill development.

SCHOOL INTERVENTIONS THAT WORK

> *The first level of intervention, however, is always through teacher-initiated regular classroom modification.*

There are no sure-fire recipes for schools to follow for reading intervention programs that will work with every child. Successful interventions depend on the needs of the individual children, the level of sophistication that teachers have for teaching reading, the resources that are available to the school, and accurate assessment of the reading deficit. The first level of intervention, however, is always through teacher-initiated regular classroom modification.

Classroom Modifications

Most students who are struggling to read are initially helped in their regular classroom. This is the type of student support that was provided in the Washington model through Tier 1 interventions. Reading instruction for students who are just slightly below expected reading levels may be enhanced as teachers identify specific difficulties and introduce instructional strategies to overcome them. Teachers may also select from value-added materials that provide additional practice with the same concepts that the whole class learns for students who are not making adequate progress. When supplemental materials are not built into reading programs, teachers need to develop additional activities for students to practice emerging skills. In this way, classroom modifications can change the amount of time spent on each skill, provide additional materials, or revise instructional methods. Interventions selected by the teacher that modify classroom instruction are frequently appropriate for students who are English language learners and for students who qualify for special education services.

Supplemental Instruction

Students with more severe reading problems need a direct-instruction reading program to supplement regular classroom instruction. This type of intervention must be based on careful evaluation of the child's individual reading deficiency. Deficiencies may occur in the areas of cognition, decoding, comprehension, or fluency. Because children can have deficit skills in more than one area, supplemental programs must be designed to correct all deficit areas if the child is to become a fluent reader. The classroom teacher, language speech pathologist, or reading specialist can provide supplemental regular reading instruction. The Bethel School District, in the intervention program described previously, successfully used a supplemental intervention program with a highly scripted instructional base.

One study in Houston and Tallahassee focused on value-added direct reading instruction. It was designed to provide groups of three to five students with intensive "double dose" instruction. Each day, children received 45 minutes of instruction in addition to their regular classroom reading program. The daily lessons followed strands for decoding, fluency, and reading comprehension. All children made impressive gains. The researchers surmised that the method of instruction pales in importance when the instructional content is precisely defined, relates to the child's assessed needs, and is intensive, interactive, and consistent (Mathes, 2003).

Match the Child and the Program

Educators need to know what interventions to use with which children at what grade level and for what purpose. For example, teachers and parents do not need to be alarmed if a first-grade child is not reading with fluency. However, they do need to pay attention when a third grader reads haltingly. Likewise, it is unreasonable to expect all first graders to decode words, read, and demonstrate comprehension of text. Third-grade students need to read fluently and understand what they have read. A second-grade child is expected to use phonics' rules to write and to drop "invented spelling" that was accepted the year earlier.

Grade-level guidelines define reading skill expectations (see Table 7.1). When a child does not achieve at expected levels, there are three options:

Provide additional instruction within the regular reading program.

Supplement instruction in tandem with regular classroom reading instruction.

Implement a stand-alone reading intervention program (a complete and intensive reading program, administered during an extended reading period).

The third option is appropriate for students who are English language learners or students who have serious reading problems and are in fourth grade and above (California Department of Education, 2000b).

Table 7.1   Expected Skill Attainment per Grade Level

	Kindergarten	First	Second	Third
Cognitive Skills	X	X	X	X
Phonological Processing		X	X	X
Comprehension			X	X
Fluency				X

Note: X indicates skills expected to be mastered and the grade children are most likely to show competent performance.

Teachers serve students effectively when they base instructional decisions on assessment data and then match the strategies or program specifically to the individual needs of each student. Supplemental intervention programs are heavy-duty instructional programs. A child who is experiencing comprehension difficulties may be competent with decoding, but may need a program designed for vocabulary development and strategies to comprehend and analyze appropriate grade-level text. Similarly, a child who reads slowly may know all the rules for decoding and be able to understand text, but be unable to process text rapidly. Not all intervention programs are created for the same purpose. Children who do not develop reading skills to advance with their classmates need supplemental instruction that matches their needs.

> *Not all intervention programs are created for the same purpose.*

There are many reasons a child's brain may not be performing the tasks for reading at expected levels. The following noninclusive list of intervention programs has been reviewed for four reading deficit areas: cognitive function, decoding, comprehension, and processing speed. Contact information for the programs can be found in the Instructional Resources. It is highly recommended that educators review these or any other programs for their most current research information to determine positive student performance results from studies collected by individuals not sponsored by the publishing company.

Cognitive Function

Classroom interventions are listed in Chapter 5 and include teaching memory, attention, concentration, and organization skills. Although many games have activities that help improve cognitive function, no commercial programs were found that are designed exclusively to develop this area of reading development.

Decoding

Earobics (steps 1 and 2), Fast ForWord, Lindamood Phonemic Sequencing (LiPS), Phonemic Awareness in Young Children: A Classroom Curriculum,

Reading Mastery (levels I and II), Teach Your Child to Read in 100 Lessons, Language Tune-Up, Alphabetic Phonics, Waterford Early Reading Decoding Program, Leapfrog Literacy Center, Interactive Phonics Readers, Road to Code: A Phonological Awareness Program for Young Children.

Comprehension

Visualizing and Verbalizing, Read Write & Type, Destination Reading, Little Planet Literacy Series, Reading Mastery (level III), Waterford Early Reading Comprehension Program, Alphabetic Phonics.

Processing Speed

Fast ForWord, Seeing Stars, Scholastic Fluency Formula, Read Naturally, Waterford Early Reading Fluency Program, read and re-read as an informal classroom practice, and practice with Random Automatized Naming Charts (discussed in Chapter 9).

Instructional programs, regardless of quality of the materials, cannot be implemented successfully without a knowledgeable, expert teacher in the classroom. The reading challenge is to close the gap between what research tells us is needed for struggling readers and what is provided in our schools. Teachers want to be effective, but if they lack effective preparation to teach reading, do not understand how children learn to read, have inadequate teaching materials, or lack school-level support, they may be unable to help children who are chal-

> *The reading challenge is to close the gap between what research tells us is needed for struggling readers and what is provided in our schools.*

lenged by reading demands. Professional development support for primary teachers, and for all teachers who provide reading instruction, is our best protection to prevent children from becoming *curriculum causalities.*

REFLECTIVE QUESTIONS

1. Educators believe it is urgent that children at risk for reading failure be assessed and receive intervention promptly. What leads educators to take this stand?

2. Some children enter school with a small oral vocabulary. Why is oral language development so important to the reading process, and how can teachers respond to the needs of children with vocabulary weakness?

3. What are some important considerations for reading instruction for children who are English language learners?

4. Explain some ways in which children are assessed for the development of reading skills? What skills could be screened for kindergarten students? What additional assessments might be helpful for first- or second-grade children who are not successful readers after modifications have been made to regular classroom instruction?

5. If you are reading this book as part of a study group, describe one or more interventions for a school to implement that are responsive to the needs of all children, particularly those who are unsuccessful readers.

6. How would you decide whether to recommend a reading intervention for a second-grade child who can decode words and comprehend text but is not able to read fluently?

Comprehension and Vocabulary

8

Challenges for Second Grade

A visitor to any second-grade classroom will see many similarities to the first-grade classroom across the way. However, the urgency of learning how to decode text has settled into more specific objectives such as learning spelling patterns, multiple-syllable words, and the more irregular features of English. The classroom speaks to the overriding objective for second grade—to learn to read fluently, accurately, and with comprehension. The frontal lobes are called on to coordinate thought processes that are progressively more expansive. Think about the mind expansion that happens as children seek new understanding, build extensive reading vocabularies, make more complex neural connections to expand memory chunks, and expand connections among thoughts and concepts in novel and exciting ways.

> *Think about the mind expansion that happens as children seek new understanding, build extensive reading vocabularies, make more complex neural connections to expand memory chunks, and expand connections among thoughts and concepts in novel and exciting ways.*

READING AND LANGUAGE ARTS GUIDELINES FOR SECOND GRADE

In second grade, word decoding guidelines require that children learn word patterns, decode multisyllable words, and learn about speech conventions. Teachers provide instructional activities that also include:

writing and writing applications

written and oral English language conventions

listening and speaking strategies

organization of oral communication

speaking conventions.

While decoding continues, the expectation for this year in school is that children will go beyond the mechanics of decoding as they expand all areas of the language arts curriculum and learn to comprehend the meaning of the text that they read for themselves.

In this chapter, we focus on reading comprehension and in Chapter 9 discuss fluency. What comes first in reading development, comprehension or fluency? There are those who argue that children must be fluent readers to comprehend what they are reading. The fluent reader's brain automatically processes the underlying connections among the reading structures and is free to devote full attention to the meaning associated with the words. Reading researchers generally agree there is a strong correlation between how fast children read text and how well they are able to understand it (National Reading Panel, 1999; Shaywitz, 2003).

Comprehension, the other part of this equation, is tied explicitly to vocabulary knowledge. Steven Stahl (1999) bases his support for the relationship between the difficulty level of vocabulary and the ability to understand text on evidence from correlational and experimental studies and readability research. The answer to the question of what comes first, comprehension through vocabulary development or speed of processing text, fluency, is

> *The answer to the question of what comes first, comprehension through vocabulary development or speed of processing text, fluency, is neither.*

neither. Both appear to be developed simultaneously as a child becomes a proficient reader; furthermore, these reading skills are dependent on each other.

INSTRUCTIONAL MATERIALS FOR YOUNG READERS AND LISTENERS

Our focus on instructional strategies for teaching comprehension looks first at instructional materials. Many teachers are required to use adoptions provided by state or local districts and make instructional decisions about which parts of units to use, how to pace lessons, what skills to emphasize with which groups of students, what supplemental materials they will use and how. In other districts, teachers work with literacy coaches and use materials selected by themselves, in school teams, or by their districts. Considerations for instructional materials, presented in this chapter, include the use of illustrations, the importance of informational reading contexts, helping children to chunk information for storage in memory and retrieval, and reading levels for recreational reading.

The Illustration Trap

Why would second-grade teachers be cautioned about using material with pictures for read-aloud stories, books, or other reading materials? In pre-reading and early reading experience, as we have seen, illustrations can be wonderful lures that invite children into the world of text. However, as children become readers, teachers must also become sensitive to the possibility that illustrations take away from the students' ability to comprehend text. Children's brains are curious and demanding. They constantly try to make sense out of their experiences. When teachers read aloud to students and show pictures to augment the written words, children tend to pay attention to the pictures, because it is easier to look at the pictures than to concentrate on the meaning of what is being read.

The brain usually responds to the sensory stimuli that are easiest to understand. When illustrations are vivid and inviting, children tend to ignore the linguistic content of the story and rely on pictures to provide responses to comprehension questions (Beck & McKeown, 2001). Text with pictures may inhibit the way children access background information from their own memory systems. Accessing stored information is essential for children to create their own internal, meaningful pictures. Teachers can encourage their students to self-reflect and visualize by withholding pictures until children have responded to questions about the text. Some publishers provide text without pictures for reading practice. These materials are useful to practice fluent reading and to engage the student in creating self-generated understanding. Another concern with illustrations occurs when pictures are not representative of the text content. When illustrations are used concurrently with children's reading assignments or listening activities, teachers can be careful to use stories or books with pictures that specifically represent text and are not in conflict with the story's content.

Lack of Informational Text

Some educators criticize basal readers for relying too heavily on fictional stories, claiming that young children need a far greater exposure to text that helps them to understand the world around them (Duke, Bennett-Armistead, & Roberts, 2003). Young readers are not so far removed from early childhood when the whole world was new. They are still eager learners about animals, airplanes, and stormy weather, to name a few of the broad range of topics that interest them. In addition, children, even in the early grades, may be expected to follow signs, read instructions, heed warnings, and use newspapers, magazines, and books that are available to the public in general. Yet, classroom reading materials do not generally respond to this reading need. In addition to the need for reading exposure beyond narrative text, exposure to informational texts beginning in first or second grade can pique children's interests and curiosities. Of equal importance, text based on information about the natural or social world prepares students for the demanding work of the later grades when grade-level expectations include understanding and using informational text.

We learn just how alarmingly scarce informational text is in the first grade from a study conducted by Nell K. Duke (2000) of Michigan State University. First, we look at the terminology used by Duke for this study. *Informational* texts are generally those that intend to communicate information about the world, presumably from someone more knowledgeable than the reader, which contain

> *We learn just how alarmingly scarce informational text is in the first grade from a study conducted by Nell K. Duke (2000) of Michigan State University.*

factual content and technical vocabulary and have consistent repetitions of a topical theme. Indexes and diagrams or other graphical elements are frequently included in text that is informational in nature. The researcher also identifies two additional types of informational text. *Narrative-informational* writing provides information about the natural or social world, yet is written with linguistic features, such as books in the popular Magic School Bus series. When information about the natural or social world is conveyed through verse, it is *informational-poetic.*

In Duke's study, data from 20 first-grade classrooms in the Boston metropolitan area, representing both low and high socioeconomic groups, were collected throughout the school year. Each classroom was visited for 4 full days. Observers reported on the types of text evidenced on the walls and other classroom surfaces, in the class library, and in written language activities. The results of the study indicated that not only was there a relative absence of informational texts in the classroom print environment, but that a mean of only 3.6 minutes per day was spent on informational text–type activities during classroom written language periods. The amount of time was generally more limited for children from classrooms in low socioeconomic areas (Duke, 2000).

Informational text expands background information and builds knowledge networks. The rationale for using texts with information moves beyond the notion that children are interested and likely to pay attention. For vocabulary evolution and linguistic enhancement, teachers can explore factual information with their classes. Using factual, concrete vocabulary, children are able to classify, categorize, and define new vocabulary. For problem solving, contrasting, and comparisons children can draw upon facts, ideas, and concepts from non-narrative text.

Building Knowledge Networks

Reading comprehension moves beyond the mechanics of learning to read. We are aware that children's brains make new neural connections as they store information from classroom instruction, their experiences, and the environment in which they live. As children are exposed to new information, they unconsciously search long-term memory systems to bring previous, similar experiences to working memory to consider, use, and connect to as they make sense of the new information.

Knowledge Base and Life Experiences

Children who have had a wealth of life experiences have stored information that they can expand on to build an even bigger and stronger knowledge base. Children from middle- to high-income families are more likely to build much of this initial knowledge base from their family experiences, while children from low-income families depend more heavily on school experiences to establish this knowledge base. Reading texts in the early grades are a logical place to introduce informational texts and narrative stores laden with core knowledge. This imperative falls to teachers, as publishers of widely used reading programs appear to fail to provide enough reading experiences or teacher lessons to make up for the limited word and world knowledge experienced by children from low-income families (Walsh, 2003).

Chunking

Children develop a base of knowledge when they learn new information and attach it to information previously stored in neural networks. To accomplish holding more and more related information in working memory, the brain generally tries to organize facts, concepts, and ideas into meaningful chunks of information. In Chapter 3, we discussed the concept of chunking, and indicated that people can hold only a limited amount of unrelated information in working memory and then only for a short time. The number of information pieces we can retain is related to age. Young school-aged children may be able to hold only three or four pieces of information in working memory.

Chunking is the process of combining several pieces of information into a single item that occupies one slot in working memory. We have already discussed how children use chunking of letters to form a meaningful phonological pattern, or word, during decoding. Chunking a phrase or sentence allows the brain to conserve memory space, yet to develop higher-order conceptual thinking. To help a child organize information and ideas into conceptual chunks, teachers or parents can use strategies to tie new information to already acquired core knowledge. To capitalize on the brain's tendency to seek novelty, adults can add rhyme or rhythm to make information chunks firmly etched in working memory for practice and ultimately for automatic long-term storage and recall.

> *Chunking accounts for some of the differences teachers find between children who give simple responses to comprehension questions and those who respond in detail using a wealth of available, previously stored background information.*

Chunking accounts for some of the differences teachers find between children who give simple responses to comprehension questions and those who respond in detail using a wealth of available, previously stored background information. The information-rich children have developed the ability to make multiple connections from the words they read and to chunk information while they contemplate it in working memory (Hirsch, 2003).

Hard Reading Materials

Reading can be hard or easy, depending on the relationship between the capabilities the child has to read the words, the knowledge or experience base required for the text to be understood, the level of commitment the child has to read the selection, and the complexity of the written style. Let's assume a child not only wants to read about dinosaurs, but also has a strong desire for more information about these prehistoric beasts. The child is well versed in the topic from previous conversations with parents, television viewing, and previous book experiences. Also, this child is considered to be a strong reader by the classroom teacher. However, if the selected book or selection has a vocabulary load with too many new terms, a linguistic structure that is more common to scientific text, and organization of ideas that appear in a different discourse or style, text can become too difficult, even to the child who is seemingly ready for more in-depth information.

Adults often prefer that children read challenging books that are full of important information, not only for classroom instruction, but also for leisure reading. Yet, if we let adult preference for magazines be our guide, suggests Richard Allington, professor of education at the University of Florida, it would appear that adults, even those with advanced degrees, do not choose leisure reading materials that are difficult or uninteresting to them. Magazines such as *Scientific American* or *The Economist* simply do not have as large a readership as *Newsweek* or *People* (Allington, 2001). If adult magazine sales indicate that more people like to read publications that have a lesser vocabulary load, require less comprehensive background information, and do not pose complex linguistic styles to

> *Adults often prefer that children read challenging books that are full of important information, not only for classroom instruction, but also for leisure reading.*

interpret, then why do educators and parents think that children will react any differently to advanced materials? Contrary to the wishes of adults, children have a higher level of reading success with greater learning and improved attitudes toward learning when they read materials that are relatively easy for recreational or leisure reading.

The issue of success rate for reading based on vocabulary loading was originally reported by E. A. Betts in the book *Foundations of Reading Instruction* (1946) and, subsequently, has been available to teachers for over 50 years. For children to read comfortably, their ability to recognize words in the reading selection needs to be at a rate that allows them to read 95 to 97 percent of the words accurately with a comprehension rate of 75 percent. Betts defined word accuracy below 95 percent and comprehension below 75 percent as frustration-level reading. Numerous studies and teacher observations validate that when reading tasks become too difficult children lose their interest in reading, are less likely to feel good about their reading, achieve poorly, and ultimately give up on reading.

How can teachers measure the appropriateness of reading materials for their students and avoid books that are simply too hard for them to read and enjoy? Allington (2001) provides one quick and easy measure. Children select a book for leisure reading. Next, they read the first page or two, depending on the number of words per page. While they read, they hold up a finger for each word that they cannot read. If they have three fingers up before they finish the page/s, then the book is most likely too hard, and they need to be encouraged to select another one, unless the topic is very interesting or important to them. In that case, the teacher can closely monitor the reading process and support the reader as much as possible.

Accelerated Reader and Lexile Framework are two popular school programs that use research-based methods to determine the readability levels for a large variety of children's books. Both use computer-assisted management systems. Accelerated Reader gives a zone of proximal development for children to ensure that readers feel challenged without being frustrated with their reading selections. The Lexile Framework characterizes each reader with a measure, called a Lexile, and forecasts the level of comprehension that the reader will be able to attain with a selected text. In each case, the programs are designed to align with state standards and often with basal readers. Books for leisure reading are also given a reading level. Equipped with this kind of detailed information, teachers and parents can help children to select books that match their individual reading skills.

BUILDING THE BRAIN FOR COMPREHENSION

The rest of this chapter centers around strategies for teachers to help their students build word and world knowledge, organize their thinking into meaningful information chunks, and experience different styles of writing and text, all of which are vital to comprehension. We visit vocabulary in many variations, speaking and listening vocabulary and reading and writing vocabulary. Further, we discuss the purpose and extent of vocabulary instruction, and, finally, strategies are provided for teachers to use to direct students toward purposeful, strategic reading.

Vocabulary Instruction

Vocabulary grows through interactions with people, activities, and books that introduce new words, ideas, and concepts. This learning does not take place from students' own reading during the initial school years, since their reading content is not as advanced as their oral language levels. Reading vocabulary does not catch up to oral vocabulary until the seventh or eighth grade (Biemiller, 2003a). However, children are eventually able to read and write words that are more advanced than the ones they use in common conversation. Classroom experiences that include read-alouds, specific vocabulary instruction, and other word and world knowledge pursuits immerse children in language arts activities that are imperative for oral and reading vocabulary comprehension and concept formation, which leads ultimately to fluent reading (Hirsch, 2003).

Speaking and Listening Vocabulary

Four distinct types of vocabulary—speaking, listening, reading, and writing—are accessed together and separately in the brain. For most children, the first two, speaking and listening, have an impressive start prior to school attendance. At school, teachers are faced with instructional considerations based on their students' broad variability in the development of speaking and listening vocabulary. Speaking and listening vocabulary development is initially dependent on childhood oral language experiences and conversations. As children advance in school, their classroom experiences and leisure reading activities expose them to more and more words, and their active vocabulary for speaking and listening greatly expands.

Vocabulary development cannot be placed on hold until the reading vocabulary catches up with the speaking vocabulary, nor can vocabulary enrichment be effectively expanded from materials that young children are able to read for themselves (Beck & McKeown, 2001). With this knowledge, teachers should select materials to read to children that are several levels above the children's own reading levels. Selections, as much as 2 years ahead of the grade level, can be used by teachers to promote vocabulary growth (Walsh, 2003).

Researcher Isabel Beck, a senior scientist at the University of Pittsburgh, and her colleagues conducted a study with 80 trade books that could be read aloud to children (Beck, McKeown, & Kucan, 2003). Three new words were selected from each story for children to learn, with children learning six targeted new words per week. Children were also exposed to many other words that they could individually select to remember.

The process Beck used to teach vocabulary is called Text Talk. The program incorporates a read, re-read, and discuss strategy. New words are taught after the children hear the story. Vocabulary instruction follows this sequence:

conceptualizing words from the story

repeating words

defining words

using words in other contexts

stimulating children's examples

saying words repeatedly

New words are maintained during successive Text Talk lessons through frequent exposures. A word wall or vocabulary chart allows children to revisit new vocabulary frequently and continually during subsequent stories. For example, the teacher may say, "Remember the word 'trouble'? How could you use that word to tell about something that happened in this story?"

Children learn vocabulary development for listening and speaking concurrently with vocabulary development for reading and writing. Oral language development will advance quickly through

> *. . . but eventually children's reading vocabularies will catch up with and advance beyond what they are able to understand through oral language activities.*

activities such as read-alouds, but eventually children's reading vocabularies will catch up with and advance beyond what they are able to understand through oral language activities.

Reading Vocabulary

Ultimately, children gain the majority of their vocabulary growth through reading. From detailed vocabulary analysis provided by Cunningham and Stanovich (1998), we realize there are large differences between the opportunities for vocabulary growth between what children hear through speech and what they are exposed to from print. New word learning for competent readers happens more rapidly through exposure to print than to exposure to conversation. From this finding, it seems likely that the varying amounts of print that students read is responsible for major discrepancies that exist for school performance among students.

> . . . it seems likely that the varying amounts of print that students read is responsible for major discrepancies that exist for school performance among students.

As we noted earlier, good instruction for vocabulary building matches the way children's brains are organized. To learn vocabulary from reading, the teacher must draw the students' attention to the word or words to be learned. Students say the word, spell the word, and learn its meaning before they encounter the word during reading. The best practice is for them to be exposed to the word again in many ways and many places after they read.

Explicit elaboration techniques can be used to hold a word in working memory. For the word "bumpy," students can make a mental picture of candy with nuts in it, tree bark, a bed with someone under the covers, or something similar. They can describe the object, structure, or person by talking, writing, or drawing, thus using visual images to hold it in working memory for an extended time. Teachers can have their classes look for targeted words in other contexts, turning vocabulary acquisition into a game of word hunt that extends from the classroom to the neighborhood and beyond. Additional activities can use games, such as student-made crossword puzzles, student drawings of target words (pictionary), or "I spy a word that means. . . ." As children become actively engaged with the word through extended practice activities, they experience repeated word exposure and increase the likelihood that they will retain the word and its meaning in long-term memory.

Writing Vocabulary

Vocabulary for writing is primarily learned during the school years. Instruction that includes specific teaching of words during reading is fortified through re-exposure to the words during writing exercises. What is described as "novice writing" in the preschool years and "invented spelling" in first grade quickly advances to independent writing as students develop larger vocabularies and expand their understanding of orthographic and syntactic patterns.

Teachers foster independent writing when they integrate reading and writing activities. We see early writing in first grade that reflects topics that have meaning to the students and represents some attempt at capitalization and punctuation. During second grade, students begin to understand that writing takes different forms, such as stories, poems, or expository writing. Specific instruction directs students to proofread for editing and revisions. Second graders begin to realize that the words they write follow orthographic patterns and rules for spelling. Third-grade students are expected to write in several different formats and to revise their writing. They produce final drafts of their work with appropriate and interesting vocabulary, and their finished product is free from spelling, grammar, or punctuation errors.

Neurologically, the writing process is very different from reading, but it relies on some of the same brain structures. During reading, the brain responds first to visual stimuli, which then are processed into thoughts with meaning. When older children compose and write, the brain is commanded to start with internal thoughts. Brain structures connect in a reverse direction from reading to select appropriate vocabulary and then produce the symbols for these words in written format. In writing, the frontal lobes direct the motor cortex to coordinate arm, hand, and finger movements, rather than to activate the mouth, tongue, and jaw as it does for speaking. A symbiotic relationship exists between reading and writing. Students read for pleasure and knowledge, and students write so they can develop their ideas and have their thoughts and ideas read by others.

> *Students read for pleasure and knowledge, and students write so they can develop their ideas and have their thoughts and ideas read by others.*

Not All Vocabulary Is Taught

Text has far too many words to teach each word that is unfamiliar to all or part of the class, and vocabulary instruction can take a lot of class time. Teachers carefully make their own choice of eight to ten new words each week or use words selected by the textbook publisher. This number is insignificant compared to the number of words students are learning and need to learn to meet grade-level expectations.

Vocabulary development, then, must take on other, more efficient strategies to learn new words. Children learn strategically to self-analyze unknown words. Teachers explicitly teach the morphology of new words through identification of prefixes, suffixes, and roots that help students to identify the word's meaning and pronunciation and to determine its part of speech. Children learn to identify prefixes (the most common ones are "un-," "re-," "in-," and "dis-") and suffixes (some with heavy use are "s," "ing," "ed," and "ly"). Words are then broken into parts—beginning, middle, and ending. Frequently, the middle part of the word is from a word family that children already know. The word "unfriendly," although lengthy, becomes identifiable when it is viewed as "un-friend-ly." Word families have the same base formation as seen with "time," "timed," "timetable," or "untimely."

> Children learn strategically to self-analyze unknown words.

Children can expand vocabulary by chunking letters in long words into morphemes that hold meaning through self-applied analysis strategies without needing explicit instruction for each new word that they encounter.

The use of context clues for reading is most effective when tied to brain-compatible techniques. Approaches that teachers use effectively with older students draw upon student prior knowledge and how words work together in sentences, syntax. Readers are encouraged to draw upon cognitive resources, what they know about phonics and morphology, and additionally to determine what makes sense for the unknown word in the particular sentence (Irvin, 2001). This expanded look at context for approaching new vocabulary can be used with younger readers to draw upon what they know, rather than relying on limited clues provided by pictures or surrounding words in text.

VOCABULARY AND THE BRAIN

How do we know when a child owns a word and has it stored for automatic recall in long-term memory? First, it is helpful to define some terminology. *Unknown* indicates that the child has no previous experience with the word. *Acquainted* indicates having some understanding, and *established* means a student can identify the word and give its meaning consistently. An unknown word carries the risk of being dropped from working memory without repeated exposure. Acquainted words are held in working memory, but have not yet moved into long-term, automatic storage. Words that are established are owned by the students and are firmly attached to a network of words, ideas, and concepts that the brain can access easily.

A definition for a single word becomes more complex when the word is a part of a phrase or new concept. A word can be stored in the brain in several ways, depending on exposure and experience with the word. The word "work," for example, can have one meaning when the child is told to "work this math problem." The meaning becomes more complex when it appears as a noun in the phrase, "A mother's work is never done." A known root word, such as "dash," can have an enriched meaning when it is used in different situations. For example, the root word "dash" could represent a written symbol, mean to move quickly, signify a small amount, or be expanded to related words such as "dashing," "dasher," or "dashboard."

Vocabulary development, as we have seen, can become an engaging part of reading instruction. Playing with words in whimsical ways through puns, exaggerations, metaphors, idioms, or cartoons captivates students (Stahl, 1999). Vocabulary development, whether it is vocabulary for speaking, listening, reading, or writing, when provided in ways that are appealing and exciting helps the child's brain to hold on to words, practice identification of words, and to sort and connect words to neural networks for ease of capture and automatic recall.

How Many Exposures to Words

The amount of exposure that a child needs to move a target word into long-term memory for automatic recall depends on whether previous neural networks are available or if they need to be developed to attach the word. Four exposures, regardless of whether it is through conversation, reading, or writing, are not enough for children or for most adults to remember a new word or to attach meaning to it (Stahl, 2003). While 12 exposures are enough for most readers, teachers find children who need to use a word 20 or more times before they are able to automatically recall it.

> *The amount of exposure that a child needs to move a target word into long-term memory for automatic recall depends on whether previous neural networks are available or if they need to be developed to attach the word.*

English Language Learners and Vocabulary Development

Earlier, we identified difficulties that English language learners have with decoding skills. Think about it this way. Phoneme awareness and phonics instruction are precise. They follow the structure of language and have rules. When a student is given systematic, explicit teaching and sufficient practice, decoding skills can be mastered. However, English learners may be able to read with phonetic correctness and yet not comprehend a word of what they have read unless they have the background or experiences to understand the vocabulary. No program can teach all the words a child needs to know at the first, third, or even at the twelfth grade.

> *Because of the difficulties that children who are English language learners may experience, these students need every minute of vocabulary development that school can offer.*

Vocabulary acquisition depends, as we have seen, on both direct vocabulary instruction and on learning how to identify and categorize new words. English learners acquire most of their vocabulary indirectly through conversation with adults, listening to adults read to them, and reading on their own (Antunez, 2002). The difficulty of vocabulary development for these children is compounded by the fact that important adults in their lives may not be English speakers. There is also a significant difference between proficiency for face-to-face communication, referred to as Basic Interpersonal Communication Skills (BICS), and proficiency needed to comprehend language in the educational setting, or Cognitive Academic Language Proficiency (CALP). Because of the difficulties that children who are English language learners may experience, these students need every minute of vocabulary development that school can offer.

STRATEGIC READING WITH COMPREHENSION IN MIND

We know that if children are to hold a rich selection of words in automatic long-term memory, they must be exposed to and interact with new words. Students' comprehension and understanding can be enhanced with structured reading opportunities that activate prior knowledge, encourage visual imaging, generate questions and predictions, and encourage thinking aloud (Allington, 2001).

With this in mind, six strategies to strengthen reading interest along with comprehension will be discussed:

text without pictures

learning frames

re-telling a story

no right and wrong answers

questioning the author

self-checking

Teachers using these dynamic comprehension strategies keep children on task during reading periods and help organize their memory systems to store and retrieve information.

Text Without Pictures

By providing decodable text without pictures, discussed earlier in this chapter with cautions, teachers activate children's previous experience and knowledge. Children read the pictureless text and then talk about what they see in their minds. Teachers prompt thinking by questions, such as, "How old was Raul in this story?" "Can you describe him?" Or, "Tell how Raul's face looked when he found out the bully was waiting for him after school?" Using informational text, for example, *Look Inside Your Brain* by Heather Alexander (1990), a series of teacher questions could be "What does your brain have to do when you button your shirt?" Or, "What are you doing right now that your brain controls without you having to think about it?" And, "Name some things that you have learned by practicing or repeating." By using this query technique, students are not influenced by interpretive illustrations that may interrupt or alter their comprehension. Questioning this way is elaborative practice that locks conceptual thinking strategies into long-term memory for automatic responses. The illustrator's pictures can be shown at the conclusion of the interaction and may stimulate even further discussion about what the artist was thinking.

Learning Frames

Ed Ellis (2001) of the University of Alabama developed another sensible and powerful approach to developing skills of understanding and idea expansion. Learning frames help organize big ideas, major concepts, and important implications. A basic frame is a series of boxes organized on a student's work paper. A key topic is identified and inserted at the top of the worksheet. Initially, the teacher directs students' thinking as two or three main ideas, each with several details, are identified and recorded. The entire process culminates with a summary statement. The resulting frame looks like a chart and often fits on a single page.

This strategy directs students to think deeply about the topic, rather than to simply identify facts. The frame technique is accompanied by robust instruction, as the teacher introduces the process for developing the frame and completes one for students as a model. With each succeeding exposure to learning frames, the teacher supplies less of the information, and the children fill in more, until students can use the frame independently. Children can use learning frames to organize a report, summarize a story or expository text, or take class notes in the upper elementary grades.

This learning frame comprehension strategy can be used as early as first grade. Learning frames appeal to the developing brain by structuring thinking, supporting connections between new ideas and previous knowledge, and developing new patterns for complex thoughts.

A companion strategy is to teach vocabulary and word concepts through semantic mapping. A map of sorts results as children brainstorm ideas and the teacher records their responses on a blackboard or overhead transparency. While the students respond, the teacher also adds words that are targeted to learn. When the brainstorming session is finished, the teacher and the class develop a map to show relationships between the words. Semantic mapping looks like a mind map with categories and is most effective when accompanied by discussion (Stahl, 1999). Framing thoughts and different semantic mapping structures can be used in tandem with the next teaching technique, story re-telling.

Story Re-telling

A comprehension skill builder, re-telling a story, requires imagining, then thinking aloud. Children, either as readers or listeners, must pay attention to a story in order to integrate meaning and reconstruct parts of the story when it is finished. Teachers using re-telling as an instructional strategy must pay as much attention to what they do to set up the story and to follow the story as they do for the actual reading. When teachers choose a chapter book, such as *Charlotte's Web*, they make the read-aloud activity meaningful when they prime student attention with questions, identifying new words, or pose ideas to think about during the reading. After children hear the chapter, they engage in discussion or another activity to demonstrate their understanding of what they heard. The focused time before and after the story demands more teacher preparation, but ensures that the experience is an efficient use of instructional time.

Children's ability to talk about complex ideas, define new vocabulary, comprehend oral and written text, and understand story structure improves when children know that they will be responsible for participating in follow-up activities. Children may be asked to talk about the story or text, act out specific parts, draw what they picture in their minds, or write about the written contents.

> *Rather than recalling what they heard, they capitalize on their own conceptual ideas.*

As children engage in these activities, they recount the reading activity in their own words. Rather than recalling what they heard, they capitalize on their own conceptual ideas. This type of work demands not only memory, but also a deep understanding of the written piece to synthesize and manipulate information. It blends comprehension from a reading experience and conceptual information from life experiences through oral language.

Questions With No Right or Wrong Answers

Moving beyond concrete, expected student responses, this more intense questioning strategy is structured by teachers to accept answers that are not predetermined. When there are no wrong responses, the only corrections a teacher may request are to incomplete answers. For this type of cognitive thinking, teachers help children use what are generally called higher-order thinking skills. In terms of building a reading brain, we know that this type of cognitive processing occurs in many different brain structures and is highly dependent on memory strategies and the ability to organize information into categories.

> *When there are no wrong responses, the only corrections a teacher may request are to incomplete answers.*

The more vocabulary words a reader has and the larger the chunks of information stored in long-term memory, the greater the potential for concept development. The better the organization of storage systems, the more intense and complete a student's response can be. Children involved in strategic thinking during reading may be asked to follow directions, such as, "Write a new ending." Or, "Think about a time that you were afraid, and tell how you worked to find a solution." Or, "The text introduced you to an animal called a mule. What do you know about mules?"

Question the Author

Another comprehension strategy teachers can use requires children to challenge what they read and question what the author has written. Children may not recognize that writers are sometimes imperfect in their understanding of a topic. Helping children to see authors as fallible or capable of making errors is a strategy used by Beck and her colleagues. They call their instructional strategy "Questioning the Author."

The technique was field tested with 14 classrooms over a 6-year period. Teachers led discussions with students that were prompted by questions such as, "What is the author trying to say in the second paragraph?" Or, "How could you word that sentence so that it makes more sense to you?" Children learned to focus more intensely on the deeper meaning of the text (Beck & McKeown, 1998, p. 48). The instructional strategies force students to surpass traditional thinking that simply looks at the literal language of text. Through an active search for meaning, children validate their own experience and knowledge and learn to become thoughtful readers who question rather than passively accept information from textbooks and other expository text.

Student Self-Checking Process

Students can be taught to use a list of questions for self-monitoring during independent reading. As early as second grade, children can learn to respond on their own to questions that the teacher posts on a chart or a bulletin board. Self-questioning begins with "understanding what I read" and continues to higher-level strategies as the year progresses. This strategy includes the following areas and inquiries:

1. Understanding what I read:
   - What and who is the story about?
   - What do I need to know more about?
   - What do I need to do with the story's information?

2. Predicting, verifying, and deciding:
   - What will happen?
   - How accurate was my prediction?
   - What information supports or changes my prediction?

3. Visualizing, verifying, and deciding:
   - Did I form a good picture?
   - How accurate was my picture?
   - What information supports or changes my understanding?

4. Summarizing:
   - What has happened so far?
   - Am I missing any important information?

5. What to do if I don't understand:
   - Stop reading and re-read.
   - Look back for details.
   - Continue to read.
   - Decide why I am confused.
   - Check to see if the reading is too difficult—do I understand almost all of the words on each page? (Allington, 2001)

Questioning with this level of progressive intensity prompts students to self-check their progress during reading and to maintain attention to their reading task.

Students Achieve at Different Levels of Comprehension

Reading comprehension is dependent on word recognition. Furthermore, vocabulary is strongly dependent on early oral language experiences. There is significant evidence that children who have decoding problems devote an inordinate amount of time and cognitive energy to the sounds of the words, so they are not able to concentrate on meaning (Goldsworthy, 1996; Hirsch, 2003; Lindamood, Bell, & Lindamood,1997).

Although some comprehension deficits spring from weak instruction, other problems result from a lack of prior knowledge. In a classroom of 20 or 30 children, there may be several who lack background knowledge about almost any new topic. Teachers use a variety of techniques to pretest children's knowledge of a new topic. As we discussed earlier, if the background experience is not there, teachers must provide the experience and prompt the development of neural connections that will allow the new information to be integrated into the brain.

As children broaden their vocabulary, develop new skills, and grasp important concepts, they progress toward increased comprehension. Children who are able to comprehend text are more likely to be accomplished at a companion skill, fluency.

REFLECTIVE QUESTIONS

1. It is suggested in this chapter that teachers occasionally withhold illustrations for some of the stories they read to students. Why would this strategy strengthen the brain's ability for comprehension?

2. Chunking information helps children to put more information into each available memory slot. How is chunking related to the development of reading comprehension?

3. Many adults prefer that children read hard, academically based books for their leisure reading. What are your thoughts on this preference?

4. If you are reading this book as part of a study group, assign four people to identify and explain four different types of vocabulary that develop during a child's early years.

5. What strategies for teaching vocabulary do you find to be most useful with your students? In what ways are these strategies brain compatible?

Third Grade 9

Putting It All Together

Third grade is the year for all the areas of reading competence to come together—cognition, decoding, comprehending, and fluency. Ideally, children master decoding during the first 2 years of formal education, then move on to develop networks of information and vocabulary for comprehension, so that by third grade children's fluency, the focus of this chapter, has improved. However, we cannot wait until third grade to address the rate and accuracy of reading, because fluency is so critical to the reading demands of upper elementary grades and beyond.

After third grade, instruction no longer focuses on learning to read. Rather, it shifts to using reading as a tool for learning, expanding children's knowledge bases and making information connections for high-level thinking, reasoning, and analysis. This is not to say that word analysis instruction does not occur in the upper elementary or middle school years. However, the emphasis on reading instruction changes. More time is spent on what is read and less time is devoted to how to read.

> . . . we cannot wait until third grade to address the rate and accuracy of reading, because fluency is so critical to the reading demands of upper elementary grades and beyond.

READING AND LANGUAGE ARTS GUIDELINES FOR THIRD GRADE

One of the expectations of our educational system is that every child will leave third grade with an enthusiasm to read and with the ability to read fluently, effortlessly, and independently. Oregon has been recognized as a leader in establishing reading standards. Reading aloud with unpracticed grade-level text at a target rate of 110 to 120 correct words per minute is a specific standard for

Oregon's students in third grade. Another goal is for children to read text fluently across all subject areas (Oregon Department of Education, 2003). While this chapter targets the development of fluency and reading processing speed, content and proficiency standards for third-grade students cover the entire range of language arts skill development. They include:

word analysis, fluency, and vocabulary development

reading comprehension and analytical reading skills

literary response with a wide range of literature

self-initiated reading

writing strategies (composition, organization, penmanship, research, editing)

exploration and understanding of language conventions for oral and written English

listening, speaking, and viewing (receiving and responding to information)

using language and technology to apply higher-order thinking skills

FACTORS AFFECTING READING FLUENCY

Attaining fluency depends on many factors, including automaticity in decoding, orthographic knowledge, and the degree to which the brain has become wired to process print information.

When students can read aloud with speed, accuracy, and proper expression, they can concentrate on the meaning of the text and are more likely to understand and remember what they read (Wolf, 2003). Children who are not fluent readers, on the other hand, must devote considerable energy to the mechanics of reading, which decreases their focus on the meaning of the text. Attaining fluency depends on many factors, including automaticity in decoding, orthographic knowledge, and the degree to which the brain has become wired to process print information.

What Is Fluency?

Fluency, which literally means *flowing*, has several components. In the context of reading, fluency means the ability to read fast (Hirsch, 2003), or to read a passage where the words are spoken without hesitation, with accuracy, with prosody, and with a lack of effort (Kame'enui & Simmons, 2001). A truly fluent reader is able to adjust the rate of reading to match the vocabulary load, the linguistic complexity of the passage, or the information that needs to be obtained from the text (Rasinski, 2000). In terms of what is happening in the reading brain, reading fluency is a product of accuracy and automaticity that accesses perceptual, phonological, orthographical, and morphological processing at the letter and word level (Wolf, 2003). Researchers agree that reading fluency is a skill that children must attain to become independent readers, and that fully developed reading fluency produces smooth, relatively effortless oral reading that is accurate and has an appropriate rate, correct stress, intonation, rhythm, and word emphasis.

> *In the context of reading, fluency means the ability to read fast (Hirsch, 2003), or to read a passage where the words are spoken without hesitation, with accuracy, with prosody, and with a lack of effort (Kame'enui & Simmons, 2001).*

Orthographic Knowledge

Let us begin with an understanding of orthography. Students' brains, when structured to organize words in orthographic categories, are able to establish visual patterns within written language. They recognize graphemes that represent the sounds of language and are adept at automatically processing words for their structure and for their meaning. As students become familiar with the orthography of language, not only are they able to recognize words that appear with high frequency, but they can also quickly process less familiar words as well.

> *As students become familiar with the orthography of language, not only are they able to recognize words that appear with high frequency, but they can also quickly process less familiar words as well.*

The more times a child sees and recognizes words or word combinations, the more likely those words will be instantly identified, allowing reading to become automatic and fluid. However, children do not achieve automaticity with reading solely from constant word exposure. In fact, we prefer that most words not be learned by sight or memorization, as this method for word recall creates a false sense of reading ability. For children to process print with fluency, they begin their journey to become fluent readers by developing an understanding of the

> *In fact, we prefer that most words not be learned by sight or memorization, as this method for word recall creates a false sense of reading ability.*

orthographic system that governs words. Fortunately, the orthographic rules for English are reliable and can be taught.

Phonological processing, teaching predictable patterns in their written format, is at the very foundation of reading fluency. Beyond simple phonemes and graphemes, the positions of different graphemes and syllables, particularly at the beginning and at the end of words, are taught through phonics instruction. As children address more complex words, they learn to focus on syllables and come to understand how stress on one syllable rather than another affects word meaning (Abbott, 2001). All the instruction for phoneme awareness, phonics, spelling, and writing in the previous years comes together as children address text with multisyllable words and long sentences. Proficient readers look at each phoneme and syllable that makes up each word, but pause for none, as they automatically recognize words for their orthographic properties and continue effortlessly reading with speed.

THE BRAIN'S RATE OF PROCESSING

Researchers and reading experts generally agree that three principles have important implications for children's reading comprehension—reading fluency, vocabulary, and domain knowledge. Vocabulary and domain knowledge were discussed extensively in Chapter 8. Here we will focus on their influence on the speed at which the brain processes words when children read.

Some Children Are Fast Processors; Some Are Not

We believe that decoding ability is an indicator for success in reading. Whether it is called phonological processing, decoding, or word attack, the basic skill is being able to put sounds (phonemes) to letters (graphemes) and to apply phonetic rules to recognize words fluently, automatically, and accurately. Theoretically, children who understand the rules for decoding and can produce the sounds of phonemes will be good readers.

> *. . . researchers have identified another skill that, when accessed efficiently, works in tandem with phonological processes.*

However, researchers have identified another skill that, when accessed efficiently, works in tandem with phonological processes.

This skill, rapid automatized naming (RAN), is the ability to look at symbols, such as colored squares or simple objects, and to rapidly identify them. Reading experts believe that RAN is a very good indicator for reading success. In fact, researchers have recently found that speed of naming, rather than accuracy of naming, differentiated between people who were good readers and those who were labeled as dyslexic (Wolf, Bowers, & Biddle, 2000). Researchers emphasize that when a child lacks skills for automatic naming, comprehension, and speed of word calling, reading suffers.

> *This skill, rapid automatized naming (RAN), is the ability to look at symbols, such as colored squares or simple objects, and to rapidly identify them.*

One area for future research will be to test the hypothesis that the rate of processing and automaticity of responses are the overarching skill development area and that phonological processing is actually a component of the rate of processing. For example, when children respond to a simple perception task, such as pointing to the color red, there is no significant difference in rate of response between children who are impaired readers and children who are normal readers. However, when children are asked to identify a picture of a common object, recognize the object, determine the name of the object, say the name, and move as quickly as possible to the next object, differences in timing between the two groups—good readers and poor readers—becomes significant (Wolf et al., 2000). These tasks are usually performed with a series of symbols, numbers, colors, letters, or objects that can be easily identified by the child.

Many neurological activities are occurring rapidly and in tandem during this naming exercise. What we see the child do gives little indication of the intense activity that is happening in the child's brain. There are many points at which this brain activity can stall. While studies are still inconclusive, researchers are examining how efficient naming is affected by the ability to mentally locate

> *What we see the child do gives little indication of the intense activity that is happening in the child's brain.*

similar objects and identify the designated one, the articulation rate, and disengagement from one object to attend to the next (Wolf et al., 2000).

Assessing Reading Fluency and Automatic Naming

Reading fluency is usually assessed by measuring the speed at which text is read, followed by evaluating the quality of responses to comprehension questions. Teachers using informal reading inventories (IRIs), a graded series of passages with increasing difficulty, can identify children who process slowly when they read. More specific diagnostic information for fluency can help determine when a reading intervention is warranted. There are many tests for decoding and comprehension, but assessment of fluency has only recently begun to get the attention that it deserves as an important part of reading development.

One diagnostic tool for reading fluency is the Gray Oral Reading Test (third edition). It has 13 progressively difficult passages, each with five comprehension questions. While this timed assessment is appropriate for third graders, reading sections are leveled too high for children in the lower grades (Torgesen, 1998). Another assessment is the nationally normed Test of Word Reading Efficiency (TOWRE). One section evaluates the number of real printed words that can be accurately identified within 45 seconds. A second section measures the number of pronounceable printed nonwords a student can decode in 45 seconds (Torgesen, 1998). The Woodcock Reading Mastery Test–Revised also contains a section to assess fluency.

An early indicator of reading speed can be predicted by a less formal assessment for rapid naming of objects. The objects include colors, symbols, letters, numbers, or pictures. One simple test involves naming five different objects that are randomly assigned on a page of 50 objects. There are 10 rows of objects with 5 objects in each row. The child is directed to say an object and then to move as quickly as possible to identify the next object and so on. The amount of time, in seconds, it takes to name all 50 objects is recorded (Denckla & Rudel, 1976).

Because of the importance attached to early identification, rapid automatized naming is suggested as a part of kindergarten screening. Although teacher observation generally provides identification of children who exhibit slow processes for naming and ultimately for slow reading fluency, school psychologists most likely are able to provide an assessment for rapid naming with norms for expected naming speed. This type of assessment is useful for identification of children who, at the onset of reading instruction, show early signs of slow processing.

DEVELOPING READING FLUENCY

It takes only one painful experience with a deliberate, slow reader in a reading group to understand that the struggling reader is not likely to make the same reading progress as peers who are reading effortlessly. Teachers, in an attempt to be more attuned to the needs of these struggling readers, request that they read aloud, interrupt when a word is miscalled, and tend to give word-by-word feedback. It is interesting that students who are not fluent readers actually benefit from additional oral reading practice (Allington, 2001), yet frequently the quantity of reading they do is less, due to the difficulty of their reading material. Beyond orthographic instruction discussed earlier, a key to nurturing fluent reading is

> *It is interesting that students who are not fluent readers actually benefit from additional oral reading practice, yet frequently teachers provide less.*

to provide appropriate text and to structure successful activities where reading is fun and enjoyable (Rasinski, 2000).

All students, particularly slow, laborious readers, benefit from the three approaches that are discussed in this chapter—repetitive practice for object naming; guided, repeated, modeled oral reading; and independent silent reading at an appropriate reading level. Regardless of the strategies that teachers use, reading fluency can be strengthened through deliberate, planned reading activities.

Repetitive Practice for Object Naming

When children are fluent, accurate readers, they can devote their attention and energy to understanding what they read. We believe that rapid automatized naming is a precursor to reading with fluency. What are the implications of rapid naming for reading skill development and as a remediation technique? Practicing naming familiar objects using the same types of objects described for assessment is suggested as practice that the brain needs to speed up the rate at which objects can be identified and named. Researcher Maryanne Wolf and her colleagues have dedicated research efforts to repetitive practice for object naming. Empirical evidence of the effectiveness of this approach is anticipated.

Fluency practice can be turned into a game. Children keep a record of how long it takes to name all the objects on a chart and then attempt to improve their own times. When one set of objects, for example, colors, is mastered within a target time, the child moves on to another set, such as a chart of numbers. Each succeeding set should be mastered with quicker response times than the previous one. During this process, the brain is primed to develop facilitated neural networks for rapid identification, naming, disengagement, and movement to the next object.

Interestingly, even though flash cards for word recognition have been dubbed by some as "drill and kill," flash cards are useful for practice in reading single words. When these words, practiced with flash cards, are later found in text, children are more able to read with increased fluency (Levy, Abello, & Lysynchuk, 1997). Likewise, pictorial flash cards of objects show promise as one type of remediation practice for children with slow response rates for naming. In this case, children use flash cards with objects, pictures, or words that they already know. Students can work with partners to quiz each other, since demands to turn over the flash cards could interfere with the target process of rapid naming. The desired outcome is certainty, accuracy, and, most important, speed. Recording time and engaging children to beat their own best time provides motivation for this type of flash card activity.

Here, also, is a place where the computer is suited to provide repetitive practice. Portions of programs such as Fast ForWord or Earobics Literacy

Launch are designed specifically to present images for identification at varying speeds. Children learn to respond quickly and to prime their minds to make connections rapidly. Once the concept of naming speed is understood as a developmental skill used by readers to attain fluency, teachers can identify other classroom activities that provide this type of practice through repetition.

Read, Re-read, and Read Again

Processing speed for reading is undeniably more complex than it is for object identification. Reading puts demands on the brain structures for memory and complex recall, because reading requires both decoding skills and access to a knowledge base for comprehension. Strategies to strengthen the connections that the brain needs to access for increased reading fluency call for guided, repeated, modeled, oral reading. One way to increase reading fluency uses a re-reading strategy with 1-minute intervals. This system uses a passage that children are able to read at or above a success rate of 95 percent. The entire process uses only 5 minutes each day and begins anew at the start of each week. The technique can be used either with an entire class or with any group of students who are at a similar independent reading level. Following is the design for this strategy.

> *Strategies to strengthen the connections that the brain needs to access for increased reading fluency call for guided, repeated, modeled, oral reading.*

On the first day, the teacher reads the selected passage for 1 minute, while students follow with their own copy of the selection. Next, students read silently for 1 minute, followed by students in pairs each taking a turn to read for 1 minute. The listening partner provides corrections, as needed. Students record the last line and the last word that they read each day. This process is repeated every day for a week with the same passage. As children progress in their ability to read with fluency, the teacher monitors passages for progressive complexity. Vocabulary from the current lesson may be interjected into the target passage. Passage selection can include poetry, narrative, or instructional text. The process becomes more challenging as the teacher requires passages be read with accuracy, prosody, and attention to the meaning of the words.

Strategies for reading and re-reading can be integrated into classroom schedules as focused activities or to fill noninstructional time. Creating pairs of readers using community volunteers, cross-age tutors, peer partners, or parents (using take-home passages) provides a variety of opportunities to practice reading aloud.

In addition to the strategies described previously, the following partner read-aloud techniques are also helpful:

Set a goal, such as 85 words per minute. Students practice on their own without an audience. When they are ready to perform, they read the passage aloud to as many listeners as they can find. When the reading speed target has been reached five consecutive times, they are "signed off" for this passage.

Pair a student who is a fluent reader with a less fluent reader. Partners read a selected passage several times together until the student who is less fluent feels comfortable reading on his own. Students keep a record of accuracy and time until a target is reached, then a new passage is selected. A variation of this strategy is to pair children from different grade levels, say a second grader and a third-grade student, both who have fluency problems. In this instance, the students work together on second-grade-level passages.

Have a child read a passage into a tape recorder. The child may make the recording several times before selecting one sample to use for repeated practice. The child and teacher then set goals, such as reading with improved accuracy, decreasing time for reading, or reading with expression and prosody. The child reads along with the tape until the goals appear to have been met. At that time, another recording is made and the pre- and post-tapes are compared against the predetermined goals.

Using an echo reading approach, partner A reads a sentence. Partner B then reads the same words. This first-and-follow routine continues through the selection until each partner can re-read the passage individually at an increased rate. This technique is also used when the teacher reads and the group follows with choral reading of the same passage. A variation of this technique is to use unfamiliar, but easy-to-sing, songs. The teacher sings or says a significant portion of the lines, so the children need to read the words from the song sheet to echo the response.

Teachers can easily integrate strategies to build fluency into classroom schedules. Once attuned to the importance of providing reading practice through individual, pairs, and whole class activities, teachers can include practice for fluency on a regular basis.

Independent Reading

The last instructional technique simply, but effectively, helps children increase their reading rate through practice with silent reading at an appropriate reading level. Remember the second-grade classroom that was described in an earlier chapter. One striking feature of the class is the number of books that are available for children to read. Every classroom must be a reader's haven. School is the best place for children to get books to read, as books can be leveled, so that the difficulty of the text matches a student's ability. Evidence is conclusive that children who read more do better in school. Based on current research and what we intuitively know as educators, providing opportunities to engage all students in reading in a positive environment is both fun and productive.

Books, Books, and More Books

Literature-based instruction makes a perfect contribution to reading development to increase practice and, ultimately, fluency. When schools include activities, such as story-telling, reading aloud, poetry parties, book fairs, meeting the author events, puppet shows, writing stories, acting out stories, and other wonderfully engaging book-related activities, children learn that reading is fun.

Children can be exposed to lots of books that capture their attention in whimsical and playful ways. In the early grades, stories such as *Rain Makes Apple Sauce* invite children to play with mouth-wallowing phrases about monkeys that mumble with a jumble of jellybeans. Young children gain reading confidence with stories that have repetitive phrases, such as the everyone-is-sleeping sequence from *The Napping House.*

> Children can be exposed to lots of books that capture their attention in whimsical and playful ways.

Children find prose and poems to be appealing through authors such as Shel Silverstein. His style, which combines pictures that are a bit quirky with the unique phrases of his poetry, charm childhood audiences. Likewise, poetry with a magic twist captures the young reader's attention, for example, Dean Koontz's "The Paper Doorway." Koontz tells how it feels to be engaged and trapped within a book. Books similar to Dr. Seuss's *Cat in the Hat*, known for their appeal to early readers, are now available for primary readers as narrative-informational stories. *Oh Say Can You Seed: All About Flowering Plants* by Bonnie Worth from the Cat in the Hat's Learning Library is one such book. It contains the ever-present magic rhymes and has serious scientific information to teach, too.

We cannot resist mentioning *The Magic School Bus Explores the Senses.* This series features Ms. Frizzle, a zany, absent-minded teacher. In this story, Ms. Frizzle moves through town, while her class tries to catch up with her in the magic school bus. During the chase, the bus and the children shrink, move inside the heads of different people and animals, and learn about the senses and the brain. The Harry Potter series is yet another example of how books can capture young readers' interest. With stories like these that are laden with whimsical words, serious information, and sometimes engrossing pictures, even children who have difficulty with reading can be enticed to pick up a book for independent, pleasure reading.

Sustained Silent Reading

Sustained silent reading (SSR) was developed to provide daily time for children to be immersed in reading. SSR can be very, very good with appropriate implementation. It can be a horrid experience if it is a "drop everything and read" strategy followed by an immediate return to the previous task. This latter less-productive interpretation of sustained silent reading frequently requires students to be engaged with any available reading material and to sit quietly and read for an extended period. Teacher direction and follow-up are nonexistent. When SSR is used without an instructional intent and without any rules for implementation, it runs the risk of becoming a waste of important instructional time.

> *It can be a horrid experience if it is a "drop everything and read" strategy followed by an immediate return to the previous task.*

What practices make this reading strategy successful? Author and teacher Janice Pilgreen (2000) studied SSR with high school–aged students who were English language learners. While our target population is much younger students, Pilgreen made recommendations that speak to all grade levels:

Children need access to huge numbers of books.

Teachers are excellent models to show children how much they love to read.

A home reading program extends the time available for independent reading.

Children are not held accountable for what they read (such as having to write a book report), but time is set aside to share reading experiences and recommend books.

A sustained silent reading time may be adopted by individual teachers or adopted as a schoolwide program. In effective programs, students make selections from books that have been precoded for their individual reading level. Children, however, are given freedom to read books that are more difficult when they have interest and desire to learn more about a specific topic.

Variations to sustained silent reading could include "reading friends" who select a book together, read alone or together, and then have a conversation about their common reading experience (Hopkins, 2002). Teachers can also use sustained silent writing (SSW) by following individual reading with journal writing. SSR is a widely used strategy, intended to engage students in reading, to give them practice with materials that are self-selected yet at an appropriate reading level, and to help them get the practice they need to become fluent, confident readers.

Programs for Slow Readers

All children do not learn to read at the expected rate. First, let us define a range of expectance by grade level for how many words are read with a

1-minute timing. The first set of numbers from Shaywitz (2003) gives expected rates specifically for the *spring* of the identified grade, while the second *general* range was established by Harris and Sipay (1990) from several standardized measures:

	Shaywitz	*Harris and Sipay*
First grade	40 – 60 (spring)	60 – 90 (general)
Second grade	80 – 100 (spring)	85 – 120 (general)
Third grade	100 – 120 (spring)	115 – 140 (general)

A number of factors may influence reading rates. Although the rate of oral or silent reading may be quite similar during the early grades, for third graders the gap between reading aloud and reading silently may be significant (Allington, 2001).

In third grade, some children with slow reading rates may need instruction in the basics for phonological and orthographic processing. They may not have mastered the skills to identify, manipulate, produce, and recall speech sounds. Other children may have difficulties with reading rates due to a lack of word recognition, vocabulary, comprehension, or processing speed deficits. Unsuccessful readers at any grade level, as identified in Chapter 7, need assessment to determine a remediation plan that addresses their specific deficits. Although programs for fluency intervention or remediation are not as readily available as those that are designed for children with decoding or comprehension problems, an increasing number of commercial programs address reading fluency. One of these is the Read Naturally strategy developed by reading teacher Candace Ihnot. Read, re-read, and read again shows up again as a strategy in this program, which is designed to intervene when children are identified as at-risk students. Read Naturally includes teacher modeling, repeated reading, and progress monitoring. Teachers who implement the program use Oral Reading Fluency Norms to measure the progress made by their students.

Great Leaps is another program available at all grade levels beginning with K–2. It has remediation for phonics and sight phrases, but also includes a section on reading fluency. The intended outcomes for the fluency section are to increase speed for reading, to improve motivation, and to develop proper intonation during reading. Stories used with Great Leaps were written and designed by Kenneth Campbell, a teacher of students with learning disabilities. Stories include point of view, humor, rhyme, and rhythm as motivation for this reading intervention.

J & J readers also provide reading practice with decodable text that resembles chapter books but are engaging and appropriate for any age student. These readers are a part of a total reading intervention program called Language! (second edition), but can be purchased separately. Comprehension, language expansion, and higher-level thinking activities are emphasized with a multi-ethnic cast of characters. While the J & J readers are not part of a reading-specific program, use of these decodable books or other leveled readers can be built into an instructional plan for increasing reading fluency.

Finally, we mention Fluent Reader, which is part of the Accelerated Reader series. Fluent Reader programs, beginning with grade 1, determine students' fluency levels through a computer program. Students practice reading with a variety of reading text that can be delivered to the student with three varying speeds.

FINAL COMMENTS

Students who read slowly and lag behind their peers for reading fluency, students who receive special education services, or those who are in English learner programs should be considered and planned for in the school's reading program. Although children who are struggling readers may receive supplemental help or may receive the services of an intervention program provided on a pullout basis, they still need the benefit of a complete reading program—not a skill development program only—with their normally progressing peers.

> *Although children who are struggling readers may receive supplemental help or may receive the services of an intervention program provided on a pullout basis, they still need the benefit of a complete reading program—not a skill development program only—with their normally progressing peers.*

All primary-aged children benefit when they are a part of the rich and varied classroom conversations that happen naturally between their peers and teachers during reading/language arts instruction. Teachers are the critical force to structure school environments where children construct their reading brain and their attitude about themselves as readers. Talented teachers orchestrate a delicate balance between instruction and student engagement with learning through conversation, practice activities, reading narrative and informational texts and leisure selections aloud and silently, and through writing experiences that are shared with the class. In a school environment where teachers base their instructional decisions on how children learn to read, children are able to become fluent efficient readers. Reading competencies attained from kindergarten through third grade are critical for all aspects of education in all of the school years that follow.

REFLECTIVE QUESTIONS

1. How do you define reading fluency? From your experience, what skills need to be developed before a child can read fluently?

2. Fluent, accurate reading depends on a child's understanding of orthography, the visual patterns of written language that feature graphemes, phonology, and semantics. Describe some ways a reading program can build teaching orthography into lessons for students in the third grade.

3. Prepare a list of strategies to share with parents that would help children to increase their reading fluency. What could you tell parents to help them understand what needs to happen in the brain for a child to become a fluent reader?

4. If you are reading this book as a part of a study group, have each member explain something known about the reading brain that helps us to understand how children are able to read with automaticity, accuracy, and fluency.

Conclusion   10

Anyone who has ever been involved in a construction project knows that it's rarely a simple process. The plans need to accurately convey your vision of the final project, the materials must be available and reasonable, the builder must be skilled, and the cost must be within your means. If there are no unexpected factors—and there always seem to be—the final product will meet the needs for which it was designed, and you will feel the effort and time were well spent.

Building the reading brain is also a construction process and, as in building an edifice, many steps are involved and many factors need to be controlled for the final product—the child's brain—to become one that reads accurately, with fluency and with enjoyment. In this final chapter, we will summarize our views of what has been learned from educational research, the practice of teachers, and, more specifically, the research from cognitive science and the neurosciences about how to best build the reading brain.

Some of what we've learned comes from scientific brain research about neural structures and their functions while others deal more with information gleaned from reading research and practice. However, even though particular findings may come from research or experience outside the field of neuroscience, the information about the brain and how it learns is helping us to understand why certain instructional processes and strategies are more effective than others. For as Dr. Marian Diamond of the University of California at Berkeley is fond of stating, the more we understand the human brain, the better we'll be able to teach it (M. Diamond, personal communication, 2001).

1. The brain is not innately wired for reading; there are no naturally designated neural mechanisms for reading. The brain must co-opt structures designed for other purposes.

   Children are born with a brain that has a built-in pathway for language. If they are exposed to a language, barring any neurological

151

disability or disorder, they will learn to speak that language with little difficulty. The same is *not* true of reading. In a sense, reading is an unnatural act for the brain. There is no built-in pathway for reading. While raising children in print-rich environments is important— especially in the early years—most children do not learn to read through exposure; they must be taught.

2. Neuroplasticity is a characteristic of the brain that allows it to be shaped by experience.

   How can a brain not wired for reading eventually accomplish this extremely difficult task? The answer lies in a unique characteristic of the brain called *neuroplasticity.* The reason we can learn habits and skills that are not innate is that the brain is "plastic" throughout life. This means that it can adapt to new circumstances and require-ments, literally changing the function of certain cells. This ability to adapt to its environment, to sculpt itself depending on the demands of the environment, is one of the most amazing characteristics of the brain.

3. Difficulty in learning to read (e.g., dyslexia) can be the result of one of several factors.

   Some reading problems are the result of a neurological "glitch" in the reading pathway of the brain. This problem either can be a genetically programmed error—generally an underactivation in the angular gyrus and Wernicke's area—or may be more environmentally influ-enced, a lack of early stimulation. Other problems seem to stem from socioeconomic, ethnic, and/or second-language factors. Regardless of the source of the reading problem, nearly all deficits can be overcome with appropriate direct, explicit instruction.

4. Essential to learning to read is the understanding that the sounds (phonemes) of spoken language can be represented by print, and that a few phonemes can be arranged to make many different words.

   We call this understanding *phonemic awareness,* and whether children pick up this understanding on their own or whether it is taught explic-itly, it appears to be essential to decoding print, to learning to read. In addition to phonemic awareness, children must be able to recognize and produce rhymes, break words into syllables, distinguish parts of syllables (onsets and rimes), and determine roots or prefixes of words. *Phonological awareness* is the umbrella term given to this broader array of skills and usually includes phonemic awareness.

5. Recognizing whole words (and eventually some phrases) automatically is essential for fluent reading and comprehension.

As children become more proficient in decoding print, they begin to see common groups of letters as words. How does this happen? When a certain configuration of letters is processed numerous times, the brain begins to store this configuration as a single bit of information, a word. This chunking process is how the brain overcomes its limited processing space. Without this ability, there would be insufficient "space" in conscious memory for comprehension of what is being read.

6. Because we read for a purpose, comprehension can be considered an end product of reading.

As important as developing the ability to decode print is, it is not of much use if we do not comprehend what we read. In order to comprehend what is being read, children's brains must be able to decode automatically and unconsciously so that the conscious processing functions of the brain are totally available for understanding the content of the print. However, this does not mean that we should wait until all decoding is automatic before addressing comprehension. Reading to children and checking for their understanding of what they have heard can be done from a very early age.

7. Many factors have been shown to be strong predictors of eventual reading success.

Because language is a precursor to reading, the size of children's vocabulary, their expressive language, recognition of the letters of the alphabet and the ability to name the letters rapidly, and their knowledge of the purposes of books are all key predictors of later reading success. Reading aloud to children with interactive dialogue is one means to help children develop these skills and is therefore also a key factor. In addition, experience in writing supports the development of skills that will be important in learning to read. Listening to and repeating nursery rhymes and songs are excellent ways to develop children's emerging literacy.

8. Children's brains often need assistance in learning to pay attention to, organize, and concentrate on information as well as other factors that serve as precursors to reading.

In a sense, learning to pay attention, organize, and concentrate can be considered priming skills. When these skills are taught and supported in the classroom, children are more successful in learning to read.

Teachers also affect students' motivation and how well they store and retain information by the types of instructional strategies they employ.

9. Some strategies commonly used to teach children to decode have proved to be less effective than others. Information on how the brain learns best can assist teachers in selecting the most brain-compatible strategies.

Many earlier phonics programs used rote rehearsal strategies that were inappropriate. While children need to practice certain word forms to get them to the automatic level, the content they are practicing needs to make as much sense as possible as the brain seeks patterns. Many commonly used word walls, letter-to-sound approaches, and orthographic rules seemingly have no patterns and are confusing to the young child's brain.

10. Early assessment in kindergarten has proved to be effective in determining which children are ready to read and which ones will need interventions.

The conventional wisdom has been that some children are ready to read in kindergarten while others won't be ready until later, indicating that we should wait until they are ready. This understanding now appears to be incorrect. Instead, we now understand that many factors play a role in whether or not children appear to be ready to read. Children who have limited exposure to print, who have not been read to or learned nursery rhymes, and so on may enter school without the emergent literacy skills necessary to learn to read. Neurological factors may also play a role. Early assessment and identification of these environmental and biological factors is essential to designing the appropriate reading instructional program for all children.

11. The size of children's vocabulary and their comprehension of what they read are highly dependent on their experiences.

Comprehension of what is being read is tied very closely to children's vocabulary knowledge. Recall that the brain sculpts itself based on what it experiences. Children who have a wealth of experiences and a well-established vocabulary are much more likely to comprehend what they read. Comprehension and vocabulary, which are dependent on each other, appear to be developed simultaneously as a child becomes a proficient reader. There are many ways for teachers to build and strengthen children's vocabulary and comprehension.

12. Attaining fluency and comprehension in reading by the end of the third grade is the ultimate goal of reading instruction.

When children can read with speed and accuracy (fluently), they are able to concentrate on the meaning of the text. However, if they must devote considerable energy to the mechanics of reading, their focus on the meaning is decreased. The ability to read fluently is dependent, therefore, on how automatic decoding is, how familiar children are with the orthography of language, and how well their brains have become wired to process print.

Finally, we repeat what we stated in the introduction to this book: reading well is more than a legislated priority, it's an ethical and professional imperative. It is our hope that this book will provide an understanding of the complex reading process and be a guide to both parents and teachers as we strive to give our children the reading legacy they deserve.

Glossary

Alphabetic principle The basic understanding that segments of speech are represented by letters.

Angular gyrus A brain structure located at the junction of the occipital, parietal, and temporal lobes. It is here that the letters of written words are translated into the sounds of spoken language.

Arcuate fasiculus A band of neural fibers connecting Wernicke's area with Broca's area.

Auditory memory The ability to listen to sounds or words, hold them in working memory, and complete a task, such as repeating a string of words or putting the sounds together to make a word.

Automaticity The ability to perform a skill or habit automatically or unconsciously.

Broca's area The central region for the production of speech and processing of syntax. It is generally located in the left hemisphere.

Cerebral cortex The deeply folded outer layer of the cerebral hemispheres that is responsible for perception, awareness of emotion, planning, and conscious thought. Also called the neocortex.

Comprehension The process of attaching meaning to written or spoken language by accessing previously stored experience or knowledge.

Concepts of print The understanding of written language, including reading from left to right, from the top to bottom of the page, that spaces separate words, and that writing conveys a message.

Corpus callosum A large bundle of myelinated fibers (axons) that connects the left and right hemispheres of the brain.

Cueing systems Processes that indicate what a word or group of words is and includes use of semantics, syntax, and graphemes.

Decoding The ability to recognize a sound-symbol relationship when translating a written word to speech or to decipher a new word by sounding it out.

Dialogic reading A nontraditional adult/child reading activity where the adult asks questions, prompts the child for additional information, and describes pictures.

Dyslexia A cognitive deficit relating to phonological processing, particularly the ability to decode and recognize words.

Emergent literacy Skills that begin to develop during early infancy through meaningful activities with adults and include oral language, print knowledge, and phonological processing.

Encoding Writing and spelling words using sounds to attach to letter patterns.

Explicit instruction Programs that provide precise, systematic directions for teaching.

Expository text Written selections that include essays, paragraphs, textbook chapters, professional articles, and newspaper editorials that are used for reading instruction.

Frontal lobe One of the four major divisions of each hemisphere of the cerebral cortex located in the front part of the brain and responsible for higher-level cognition.

Functional magnetic resonance imaging (fMRI) A technique for imaging brain structure and activity by measuring oxygen use of the cells.

Grapheme Printed representations, letters, that represent a phoneme.

Individualized instruction Instruction responsive to the unique needs of each child in a classroom regardless of the lesson setting (whole class, small group, or one to one).

Letter-sound relationship The relationship between the grapheme and its corresponding phoneme.

Lexile Two measures that forecast the level of comprehension that a reader can accomplish and the level of comprehension that a reading measure contains.

Long-term memory A term given to unconscious storage of information for long periods of time.

Morpheme The smallest unit of language that has meaning.

Motor cortex The lateral part of the frontal lobes that extends from ear to ear across the roof of the brain. It governs coordination of movement and some cognitive processes.

Narrative text A written selection that tells a story and includes children's picture books, fairy tales, short stories, fables, myths, tall tales, short stories, and novels.

Neuroplasticity The term given to the characteristic of the brain that allows it to reorganize itself by forming new neural connections and to adjust their activity in response to new situations or changes in the environment.

Occipital lobe One of the four major divisions of the cortex located in the back of the brain and responsible for the processing of visual stimuli.

One-to-one instruction Instruction delivered to one student at a time, not necessarily based on individualized learning needs.

Onsets The initial consonants or blends in the syllable; not every word has an onset.

Orthography Written language's visual patterns that account for features of graphemes, phonology, and semantics.

Parietal lobe One of the four major divisions of the cortex located in the upper back part of the brain. It is responsible for sensory integration.

Phoneme The smallest sound of speech that corresponds to a particular letter of an alphabetic writing system.

Phonemic awareness Conscious understanding that words are made of individual sounds (phonemes) from speech and that these sounds are representative of the alphabet. Phonemic awareness activities include rhyming, alliteration, oddity tasks, phoneme segmentation, phoneme blending, phoneme manipulation, and syllable splitting.

Phonetics The study of articulation of speech sounds.

Phonics A system used in alphabetic writing that is representative of speech sounds, which can be referred to as instruction for sound-symbol reading or a phonics approach to reading.

Phonological awareness Awareness at all levels of the speech/sound system, including stress patterns, onset-rime units, syllables, and phonemes. It includes both phonemic awareness and a systematic approach to phonics instruction systems.

Phonological processing An inclusive term representing the process used to identify, manipulate, produce, and remember speech sounds, which includes word pronunciation, use of memory for naming word, syllable, and rhyme, and phoneme segmentation blending and manipulation.

Phonological sensitivity Breaking the code for how written language represents oral language; an indication of the understanding that words are made up of smaller sounds, such as phonemes and syllables.

Phonology The study of rules that govern how speech is identified for individual sounds and bringing the understanding to an unconscious level.

Positron emission tomography (PET) A technique for imaging physiological activity in the brain using radioactive dyes injected into the bloodstream.

Pragmatics A rule system for communication that tells speakers how to choose words.

Print conventions Matching oral words and printed words; learning titles, authors, and conventions of books and other forms of print; and discrimination of letters, words, and sentences.

Print knowledge Understanding that words are represented by print, that letters of the alphabet are represented in different ways (e.g., upper- and lowercase letters), and that letters can represent multiple sounds or the same sound represented by different letters.

Processing speed The rate at which a task, such as reading, occurs through accessing brain structures that are developed for this function.

Prosody The stress and intonation patterns, rhythm, and emphasis given to words during oral reading.

Rhyme The correspondence of ending sounds or lines.

Rime A vowel and the following consonants that make a syllable, letter combinations previously referred to as phonograms or word families.

Semantics The meaning of words, phrases, sentences, text, as reflective of the individual's background information and experience.

Sensory memory A term given to the initial processing of stimuli coming into the brain from internal or external sources.

Source memory An attribute of episodic memory to retrieve what happened, where an incident happened, and when it happened following a highly emotional experience. Details, although vivid in the mind, may lack accuracy.

Synapse The physical structure that makes an electrochemical connection between neurons.

Syntax A rule system that functions unconsciously to order words in phrases and ultimately sentences that correspond to accepted rules for grammar.

Systematic phonics instruction A plan for teaching that is carefully designed around a set of sound-letter relationships following a logical order for introduction.

Temporal lobe One of the four major divisions of the cerebral cortex located on the sides of each hemisphere. It is responsible for auditory processing and some aspects of memory.

Visual memory The ability to receive images through the vision center of the brain and hold the images in working memory to complete a task, such as identifying a word from its letters or identifying a series of symbols.

Wernicke's area The language center responsible for comprehension of speech. It is typically located in the left hemisphere.

Word recognition Identifying groups of letters or meaningful units, morphemes, such as prefixes, suffixes, and inflectional endings to determine an unknown word.

Working memory A term given to the conscious processing of information.

Instructional Resources

Accelerated Reader, Fluent Reader Software, Renaissance Learning. www.renlearn
.com. (866) 846-7323.

Alphabetic Phonics, Educational Publishing Service. www.epsbooks.com. (800)
435-7728.

Destination Reading, Riverdeep—The Learning Company. www.riverdeep.net. (800)
382-2890.

Earobics Literacy Launch, Cognitive Concepts. www.cogcon.com. (888) 328-8199.

Fast ForWord, Scientific Learning. www.ScientificLearning.com. (888) 452-7323.

Fluency Formula and Interactive Phonics Readers, Scholastic. http://teacher.
scholastic.com/ps. (800) 724-6527.

Great Leaps, Diarmuid, Inc. www.greatleaps.com. (877) 475-3277.

Interactive Phonics Readers, Scholastic. http://teacher.scholastic.com/ps. (800)
724-6527.

J & J Readers, Sopris West. www.sopriswest.com. (303) 651-2829.

Language Tune-Up, Orton-Gillingham. www.jwor.com. (888) 431-6310.

Leapfrog Literacy Center, Leapfrog Enterprises, Inc. www.leapfrogschoolhouse.com.
(800) 883-7430.

Lindamood Phonemic Sequencing, LiPS, Lindamood-Bell. www.lindamoodbell.com.
(805) 541-3836.

Little Planet Literacy Series, Little Planet Learning. www.littleplanet.com. (888)
974-2248.

Phonemic Awareness in Young Children: A Classroom Curriculum, Marilyn Jager
Adams, Barbara R. Foorman, Ingvar Lundberg, & Terri Beeler (Baltimore: Brookes
Publishing, 1998). http://www.pbrookes.com.

Read Naturally. www.readnaturally.com. (615) 452-4085.

Read Write & Type, Educational Software Cooperative Net Ring, Talking Fingers, Inc.
www.readwritetype.com. (800) 674-9126.

Reading Mastery—Rainbow Edition, McGraw-Hill. http://sra-4kids.com. (888)
772-4543.

Road to the Code: A Phonological Awareness Program for Young Children, Benita A.
Blachman, Eileen Wynne Ball, Rochella Black, & Darlene M. Tangel (Baltimore:
Brookes Publishing). www.pbrookes.com. (800) 638-3775.

Seeing Stars, Lindamood-Bell. www.lindamoodbell.com. (805) 541-3836.

Test of Word Reading Efficiency (Towre), Joseph Torgesen, Richard Wagner, & Carol
Rashotte. www.cogcon.com/products/towre.cfm. (888) 328-8199.

Visualizing and Verbalizing for Language Comprehension and Thinking, Nanci Bell (San Luis Obispo, CA: Gander Publishing, 1991). www.lindamoodbell.com. (805) 541-3836.

Waterford Early Reading Program, Pearson Digital Learning. www.electronic education.com. (480) 840-7700.

Woodcock Reading Mastery Test—Revised, American Guidance Services. www.agenet. com. (800) 328-2560.

Words Their Way: Word Study for Phonics, Vocabulary, and Spelling, Donald R. Bear, Marcia Invernizzi, Shane Templeton, & Francine Johnston (Columbus, OH: Merrill/ Prentice-Hall, 1998). http://www.prenhall.com.

Classroom Library (limited to books referenced in text)

Moses Supposes His Toeses Are Roses, N. Patz (San Diego: Harcourt Brace Jovanovich, 1983).

Oh Say Can You Seed: All About Flowering Plants, Bonnie Worth (author), Alice Jonaitis (editor), & Aristides Ruiz (illustrator) (Cat in the Hat's Learning Library, 2001). http://www.ages4-8.com.

The Magic School Bus Explores the Senses, Joanna Cole & Bruce Degen (New York: Scholastic, 1999). http://teacher.scholastic.com/ps. (800) 724-6527.

The Napping House, Audrey Wood (author) & Don Wood (illustrator) (San Diego: Harcourt Brace, 1984). www.harcourt.com.

The Paper Doorway, Funny Verse and Nothing Worse, Dean Koontz (author) & Phil Parks (illustrator) (New York: Harper/Collins, 2001). www.harpercollins.com/.

There's a Wocket in My Pocket, T. S. Geisel (Dr. Seuss) (New York: Random House, 1974).

Rain Makes Applesauce, Julian Scheer (author) & Marvin Bileck (illustrator) (New York: Holiday House, 1985). http://holidayhouse.com.

Look Inside Your Brain, Heather Alexander (author) & Nicoletta Costa (illustrator) (New York: Grosset & Dunlap, 1998).

Family Support

Between the Lions: Get Wild About Reading, PBS Preschool Education Program: Ready to Learn. Contact for Los Angeles: (323) 953-5202.

Linda Clinard, *Family Time, Reading Fun* (2nd ed.) (Dubuque, IA: Kendall/Hunt, 2002).

Siegfried Engelmann, Phyllis Haddox, & Elaine Bruner, *Teach Your Child to Read in 100 Easy Lessons* (New York: Simon & Schuster, 1986).

Web Resources for Building a Reading Brain

http://www.pattan.k12.pa.us/Instruction/default.htm#Stages of Learning. Effective instruction is presented in a primer-type format. This Web site comes from the research and work of Edward Kame'enui, Martin Kozloff, and Doug Carnine. It has technical guidelines that range from cognitive strategies for student learning to explicit help for how to teach. A toolkit is available for in-depth information about any facet of instruction. The site contains a plethora of information for teachers at any stage of their career.

http://www.uoregon.edu/~bgrossen. A Web site through the University of Oregon, from the Center for Applied Research in Education (C.A.R.E.). This is a nonprofit organization formed by Bonnie Grossen to support schools that serve students who are at risk of failure. The C.A.R.E. team includes teachers and principals who have achieved excellent results with students who are traditionally low-achievers. This site gives up-to-date information that includes a direct instruction model for middle school students as they seek to reach academic expectations and standards.

http://idea.uoregon.edu/assessment/index.html. The Reading First legislation requires state and local educational agencies to receive assistance on the selection and use of reading assessment instruments for kindergarten through grade 3. This site gives report and presentation information from an assessment committee.

http://www.adihome.org. This site gives information about the Association for Direct Instruction. Of particular interest is the availability of articles from the *Journal of Direct Instruction.*

http://www.mcrel.org. A site dedicated to making a difference in the quality of education through applied research. A large number of resources are available that include products, services, and educator resources for content area teaching. Of particular interest is a lesson-plan library that includes the arts, behavioral/social sciences, civics, economics, health/PE, and seven others.

http://aft.org. The American Federation of Teachers sponsors this site. It includes the latest news, publications, a press center, a parent page, among others. Noteworthy is the availability of articles on research-based reading programs and instructional practices. Issues of *American Educator* are available on a quarterly basis.

http://www.allkindsofminds.org. All Kinds of Minds is an organization with a mission to help students who struggle to be successful in school. The foundation, launched in 1995, has a school-attuned program, regional training for teachers, and an active Web site and monthly newsletter. Articles and related information lead to cognitive information for clinicians, educators, and families.

http://www.coreknowledge.org. An organization dedicated to identifying core knowledge as a specific, shared content across the grades. Grade-level guides provide content that is solid, sequenced, specific, and shared. Parent information is provided in resources, such as "What Your Kindergartner Needs to Know."

http://www.crayola.com. This company offers activities for parents, educators, and "Crayola kids." A free registration is required. A guide is produced each year for teachers with lessons that encourage visual literacy, reading, writing, storytelling, and "thinking outside the box."

http://www.readingrockets.org. This Web site, provided by WETA, a public television station in Washington, DC, gives research-based information about the process of reading. There is a wealth of practical activities for classrooms and for parents to use that encourage children to do more reading, such as "Moving Into Reading: Preschool Through Grade Two."

http://www.rethinkingschools.org. Sponsored by the National Council of Teachers of English, this Web site provides different views of the teaching of reading, teaching children with diverse needs, and the efficacy of teachers.

References

Aaron, P. G. (1995). Differential diagnosis of reading disabilities. *School Psychology Review, 24*(3), 345–360.

Abbott, M. (2001). Effects of traditional versus extended word-study spelling instruction on students' orthographic knowledge. *Reading Online, 5*(3).

Ackerman, S. J. (2003). News from the Frontier, an unfelt filter. *Brain Work, The Neuroscience Newsletter, 13*(3), 7–8.

Acredelo, L., & Goodwyn, S. (1996). *Baby signs.* Chicago: Contemporary Books.

Adams, M. J. (1990). *Beginning to read: Thinking and learning about print.* Cambridge, MA: MIT Press.

Adams, M. J., Foorman, B. R., Lundberg, I., & Beeler, T. (1998a). The elusive phoneme. *American Educator, 22*(1–2), 18–29.

Adams, M. J., Foorman, B. R., Lundberg, I., & Beeler, T. (1998b). *Phonemic awareness in young children: A classroom curriculum.* Baltimore: Brookes Publishing.

Alaska State Board of Education. (1999). *Reading performance standards* [On-line]. Available: www.educ.state.ak.us/.

Alexander, A., Anderson, H., Heilman, P. C., Voeller, K. S., & Torgesen, J. K. (1991). Phonological awareness training and remediation of analytic decoding deficits in a group of severe dyslexics. *Annals of Dyslexia, 41,* 193–206.

Allington, R. (2002). You can't learn from books you can't read. *Educational Leadership, 60*(3), 16–19.

Allington, R. L. (1989). Coherence or chaos? Qualitative dimensions of the literacy instruction provided low-achievement children. In A. Gartner & D. Lipsky (Eds.), *Beyond separate education.* Baltimore: Brookes Publishing.

Allington, R. L. (2001). *What really matters for struggling readers: Designing research-based programs.* New York: Longman.

Anbar, A. (1986). Reading acquisition of preschool children without systematic instruction. *Early Childhood Research Quarterly, 1,* 69–83.

Antunez, B. (2002). Implementing reading first with English language learners. *Directions in Language and Education* [On-line], *15.* Available: http://www.ncela.gwu.edu/ncbepubs/directions/15.pdf.

Archer, A. (2000). *Expository writing.* Presentation for Sonoma County Office of Education.

Baddeley, A. D. (1979). Working memory and reading. In P. Kolers, E. Wrolstad, & H. Bouma (Eds.), *Processing of visible language* (Vol. 1). New York: Plenum Press.

Baddeley, A. D. (1986). *Working memory.* Oxford: Oxford University Press.

Baker, L., Serpell, R., & Sonnenschein, S. (1995). Opportunities for literacy learning in the homes of urban preschoolers. In L. M. Morrow (Ed.), *Family literacy: Connections in schools and communities* (pp. 236–252). Newark, DE: International Reading Association.

Barton, M. L., Heidema, C., & Jordan, D. (2002). Teaching reading in mathematics and science. *Educational Leadership, 60*(3), 24–27.

Bear, M. F., Conners, B. W., & Paradiso, M. A. (1996). *Neuroscience: Exploring the brain.* New York: Lippincott/Williams & Wilkins.

Beck, I. L., & McKeown, M. G. (1998). Comprehension: The sine qua non of reading. *The keys to literacy* (pp. 40–52). Washington, DC: Council for Basic Education.

Beck, I. L., & McKeown, M. G. (2001). Text talk: Capturing the benefits of read-aloud experiences for young children. *Reading Teacher, 55*(1), 10–21.

Beck, I. L., McKeown, M. G., & Kucan, L. (2003). Taking delight in words: Using oral language to build young children's vocabularies. *American Educator, 27*(1), 36–41, 45–48.

Bee, H. L., & Mitchell, S. K. (1980). *The developing person: A life-span approach.* New York: Harper & Row.

Bell, N. (1991). *Visualizing and verbalizing for language comprehension and thinking.* San Luis Obispo, CA: Gander Publishing.

Berninger, V. W. (2002). *Revealing the secrets of the brain: Neuropsychologist Virginia Berninger studies brain images before and after instruction for clues to the mystery of learning disabilities* [On-line]. Available: http://www.nwrel.org/nwedu/08-03/brain-t.asp.

Berninger, V. W., & Richards, L. R. (2002). *Brain literacy for educators and psychologists.* San Diego: Academic Press.

Berninger, V. W., & Whitaker, D. (1993). Theory-based branching diagnosis of writing disabilities. *School Psychology Review, 22*(4), 623–642.

Betts, E. A. (1946). *Foundations of reading instruction.* New York: American Book Co.

Biemiller, A. (2003a). *Using stories to promote vocabulary* [On-line]. Retrieved May 5, 2003, from www.reading.org/meetings/conv/conv03.news2.html.

Biemiller, A. (2003b). Oral comprehension sets the ceiling on reading comprehension. *American Educator, 27*(1), 23.

Billman, L. W. (2002). Aren't these books for little kids? *Educational Leadership, 60*(3), 48–49.

Blankenburg, F., Taskin, B., Ruben, J., Moosmann, M., Ritter, P., Curio, G., & Villringer, A. (2003, March 21). Imperceptible stimuli and sensory processing impediment. *Science, 299*(5614), 1864.

Bloom, F. E., Beal, M. F., & Kupfer, D. J. (2003). *The Dana guide to brain health.* New York: Free Press.

Bloom, P. (2000). *How children learn the meaning of words.* Cambridge, MA: MIT Press, abstract [On-line]. Available: www.spencer.org/publications/abstracts/abstract.children.learn.htm.

Bock, R. (2002). *Why children succeed or fail at reading* [On-line]. Retrieved August 30, 2002, from http://156.40.88.3/publications/pubs/readbro.htm.

Bond, G. L., & Dykstra, R. (1967). The cooperative research program in first-grade reading instruction. *Reading Research Quarterly, 2*, 5–142.

Bookheimer, S. Y., Zeffiro, T. A., Blaxton, T., Gaillard, W. D., & Theodore, W. H. (1995). Regional cerebral blood flow during object naming and word reading. *Human Brain Mapping, 3*(2), 93–106.

Brabham, E. G., & Villaume, S. K. (2001). Questions and answers: Building walls of words. *The Reading Teacher, 54*(7), 700–702.

Bredekamp, S. (1987). *Developmentally appropriate practice in early childhood programs serving children from birth through age 8.* Washington, DC: National Association for the Education of Young Children.

Bredekamp, S., & Rosegrant, T. (1992). *Reaching potentials: Appropriate curriculum and assessment for young children* (Vol. 1). Washington, DC: National Association for the Education of Young Children.

Bucuvalas, A., & Juel, C. (2002). The limitations of over-emphasizing phonics: The research of Professor Connie Juel. *HGSE News* [On-line]. Available: http://www.gse.harvard.edu/news/features/juel12012002.html.

Bus, A., Van Ijzendoorn, M., & Pellegrini, A. (1995). Joint book reading makes for success in learning to read: A meta-analysis on intergenerational transmission of literacy. *Review of Educational Research, 65*, 1–21.

California Department of Education. (1999). *Reading/language arts framework for California public schools, kindergarten through grade twelve.* Sacramento: Author.

California Department of Education. (2000a). *California 2002 K–8 reading/language arts/English language development adoption criteria.* Sacramento: Author.

California Department of Education. (2000b). *Prekindergarten learning development guidelines.* Sacramento: Author.

Caplan, D. (1995). *The Harvard Mahoney Neuroscience Institute Letter, 4*(4).

Carter, R. (1998). *Mapping the mind.* Los Angeles: University of California Press.

Center for the Improvement of Early Reading Achievement (CIERA). (2001). *Put reading first: The research building blocks for teaching children to read.* A joint publication with the National Institute for Literacy, the National Institute of Child Health and Human Development, and the U.S. Department of Education. Jessup, MD: National Institute for Literacy.

Chall, J. S. (1983). *Learning to read: The great debate.* New York: McGraw-Hill.

Chomsky, N. (1972). Stages in language development and reading exposure. *Harvard Educational Review, 42*, 1–33.

Chomsky, N. (1979). Approaching reading through invented spelling. In L. B. Resnick & P. A. Weaver (Eds.), *Theory and practice of early reading* (Vol. 2, pp. 43–65). Hillsdale, NJ: Erlbaum.

Chow, P., & Chou, C. (2000). Evaluating sustained silent reading in reading classes. *The Internet TESL Journal* [On-line], *6*(11). Available: http://iteslj.org.

Chugani, H. (1998). A critical period of brain development: Studies of cerebral glucose utilization with PET. *Preventive Medicine, 27,*184–188.

Clachman, B. Z. (1991). Phonological awareness: Implications for prereading and in literacy instruction. In S. A. Brady & D. P. Shankweiler (Eds.), *Phonological processes in literacy* (pp. 29–36). Hillsdale, NJ: Erlbaum.

Clarke, L. K. (1988). Invented versus traditional spelling in first graders' writings: Effects on learning to spell and read. *Research in the Teaching of English, 22*(3), 281–309.

Clay, M. M. (1979). *The early detection of reading difficulties* (2nd ed.). Auckland, New Zealand: Heinemann.

Clay, M. M. (1993). *Reading recovery in English and other languages.* Keynote address presented at the West Coast Literacy Conference, Palm Springs, CA.

Cummins, J. (2000). *Bilingual children's mother tongue: Why is it important for education?* [On-line]. Available: www.iteachilearn.com/cummins/mother.htm.

Cunningham, A. E., & Stanovich, K. E. (1998). What reading does for the mind. *American Educator, 22*(1–2), 8–15.

Cunningham, P., Hall, D. P., & Heggie, T. (1994). Making words, multilevel—hands on developmentally appropriate spelling and phonics. Torrance, CA: Good Apple.

Deacon, T. W. (1997). *The symbolic species: The co-evolution of language and the brain.* New York: W. W. Norton.

Denckla, M. B., & Rudel, R. G. (1976). Rapid automatized naming (RAN): Dyslexia differentiated from other learning disabilities. *Neuropsychologia, 14,* 471–479.

Diamond, M., & Hopson, J. (1998). *Magic trees of the mind: How to nurture your child's intelligence, creativity, and healthy emotions from birth through adolescence.* New York: Penguin Books.

Dickinson, D. K., Cote, L., & Smith, M. W. (1993). Learning vocabulary in preschool: Social and discourse contexts affecting vocabulary growth. In C. Daiute (Ed.), *The development of literacy through social interaction. New directions for child development No. 61: The Jossey-Bass Education Series.* San Francisco: Jossey-Bass.

Dickinson, D. K., & Smith, M. W. (1994). Long-term effects of preschool teachers' book readings on low-income children's vocabulary and story comprehension. *Reading Research Quarterly, 29*(2), 104–122.

Duke, N. K. (2000). 3.6 minutes per day: The scarcity of informational texts in first grade. *Reading Research Quarterly, 25*(2), 202–223.

Duke, N. K., Bennett-Armistead, V. S., & Roberts, E. M. (2003). Filling the great void: Why we should bring nonfiction into the early-grade classroom. *American Educator, 27*(1), 30–35.

Durkin, D. (1996). *Children who read early.* New York: Teachers College Press.

Dykstra, R. (1967). *Continuation of the coordinating center for first-grade reading instruction programs* (Report of Project 6-1651). Minneapolis: University of Minnesota.

Eden, G., Van Meter, J., Rumsey, J., Maisog, J., Woods, R., & Zeffiro, T. (1996). Abnormal processing of visual motion in dyslexia revealed by functional brain imaging. *Nature, 382,* 66–69.

Eimas, P. D., Siqueland, E. R., Jusczyk, P., & Vigorito, J. (1971). Speech perception in infants. *Science, 171,* 303–306.

Eliot, L. (1999). *What's going on in there?* New York: Bantam Books.

Ellis, E. (2001). *Makes sense strategies: Framing for success* [On-line]. Available: http://www.ldonline.org/ld_store/masterminds.html.

Farstrup, A. (2000, May 21). Reading is more than phonics. *Tallahassee Democrat.*

Fletcher, J. M., & Lyon, G. R. (1998). Reading: A research-based approach. In W. Evers (Ed.), *What's gone wrong in America's classrooms.* Stanford, CA: Hoover Institution Press.

Florida Department of Education. (2001). *Just read, Florida!* [On-line]. Available: www. fldoe.org.

Foreman, J. (2002). The evidence speaks well of bilingualism's effect on kids. *The Brain in the News, 9*(19), 3.

Francis, D. J., Shaywitz, S. E., Stuebing, K. K., Shaywitz, B. A., & Fletcher, J. M. (1996). Developmental lag versus deficit models of reading disability: A longitudinal growth curves analysis. *Journal of Educational Psychology, 88,* 3–17.

Francis, D. J., Shaywitz, S. E., Stuebing, K. K., Shaywitz, B. A., & Fletcher, J. M. (1997). Early intervention for children with reading disabilities: Study designs and preliminary findings. *Learning Disabilities: A Multi-Disciplinary Journal, 8,* 63–71.

Fuchs, L. S., Fuchs, D., Hosp, M. K., & Jenkins, J. R. (2001). Oral reading fluency as an indicator of reading competence: A theoretical, empirical, and historical analysis. *Scientific Studies of Reading, 5*(3), 239–256.

Gazzaniga, M. (1998). *The mind's past.* Berkeley, CA: University of California Press.

Gogner, D., Raphael, L., & Pressley, M. L. (2002). How grade 1 teachers motivate literate activity by their students. *Scientific Studies of Reading, 6*(2), 135–155.

Goldman, S. R., Hogaboam, T. W., Bell, L. C., & Perfetti, C. A. (1980). Short-term retention of discourse during reading. *Journal of Educational Psychology, 68,* 680–688.

Goldsworthy, C. (1996). *Developmental reading disabilities: A language based treatment approach.* San Diego: Singular Publishing Group.

Goldsworthy, C. (1998). *Sourcebook of phonological awareness activities: Children's classic literature.* San Diego: Singular Publishing Group.

Gopnik, A., Meltzoff, A., & Kuhl, P. (2000). *The scientist in the crib.* New York: William Morrow.

Greenfield, S. (2000). *Brain story: Unlocking our inner world of emotions, memories, ideas, and desires.* New York: Dorling Kindersley Publishing.

Greenspan, S., & Lewis, N. B. (1999). *Building healthy minds: The six experiences that create intelligence and emotional growth in babies and young children.* Cambridge, MA: Perseus Books.

Grossen, B. (1997). *30 years of research: What we know about how children learn to read* [On-line]. Retrieved February 2003 from http://www.cftl.org/30years/30years. html.

Hall, S. L., & Moats, L. C. (1999). *Straight talk about reading: How parents can make a difference during the early years.* Lincolnwood, IL: NTC/Contemporary Publishing Group.

Hamaguchi, P. M. (2000). *Practical therapeutic strategies for central auditory processing disorders.* Presentation to Region 10 Coordinating Council, Language and Speech Committee, Apple Valley, CA.

Harris, A. J., & Sipay, E. R. (1990). *How to increase reading ability* (8th ed.). New York: Longman.

Hart, B., & Risley, T. R. (2003, Spring). The early catastrophe. *The American Educator.*

Healy, J. (1985). *Endangered minds: Why our children don't think.* New York: Simon & Schuster.

Healy, J. (1987). *Your child's growing mind: A guide to learning and brain development from birth to adolescence.* New York: Doubleday.

Heilman, K., Voeller, K., & Alexander, A. (1996). Developmental dyslexia: A motor–articulatory feedback hypothesis. *Annals of Neurology, 39,* 407–412.

Herschkowitz, N., & Herschkowitz, E. C. (2002). *A good start in life: Understanding your child's brain and behavior.* Washington, DC: Dana Press.

Hettleman, K. R. (2003). *The invisible dyslexics: How public school systems in Baltimore and elsewhere discriminate against poor children in the diagnosis and treatment of early reading difficulties.* Baltimore: Abell Foundation.

Hirsch, E. D., Jr. (2003). Reading comprehension requires knowledge and words and the world. *American Educator, 27*(1), 10–22, 28–29, 48.

Honig, B. (2001). *Teaching our children to read.* Thousand Oaks, CA: Corwin Press.

Hopkins, G. (2002). Sustained silent reading helps develop independent readers (and writers). *Education World* [On-line]. Available: www.education-world.com/a_curr/curr038.shtml.

Hotz, R. L. (2002a, July 29). In dyslexia study, a child's reading is written on brain. *Los Angeles Times,* p. A10.

Hotz, R. L. (2002b, November 8). Neuroscientists mine the depths of emotions. *Los Angeles Times.*

Huttenlocher, J., Haight, W., Bryk, A., Seltzer, M., & Lyons, T. (1991). Early vocabulary growth: Relation to language input and gender. *Developmental Psychology, 27,* 236–248.

Illinois State Board of Education. (2002). *Illinois reads* [On-line]. Available: www.isbe.state.il.us.

Irvin, J. L. (2001). Assisting struggling readers in building vocabulary and background knowledge. *Voices From the Middle, 8*(4), 37–43.

Juel, C., & Minden-Crupp, C. (2000). Learning to read words: Linguistic units and instructional strategies. *Reading Research Quarterly, 35*(4), 458–493.

Jusczyk, P. W. (1999). How infants begin to extract words from speech. *Trends in Cognitive Science, 3,* 323–328.

Kail, R. V. (1984). *The development of memory in children.* New York: W. H. Freeman.

Kame'enui, E. J. (2002). *Analysis of reading assessment instruments for K–3* [On-line]. Available: http://idea.uoregon.edu/assessment.

Kame'enui, E. J., & Simmons, D. C. (2000). *Planning and evaluation tool for effective school-wide reading program.* Eugene, OR: University of Oregon, College of Education, Institute for the Development of Educational Achievement.

Kame'enui, E. J., & Simmons, D. C. (2001). Introduction to this special issue: The DNA of reading fluency. *Scientific Studies of Reading, 5*(3), 2003–2010.

Koralek, D., & Collins, R. (1997). *On the road to reading: A guide for community partners.* A joint project of the Corporation for National Service, the U.S. Department of Education, and the U.S. Department of Health and Human Services. Available: www.ed.gov/pubs/RoadtoRead/part2.html.

Kotulak, R. (1997). *Inside the brain: Revolutionary discoveries of how the mind works.* Kansas City, MO: Andrews McMeel.

Kuhl, P., Williams, K., Lacerda, F., Stevens, K., & Lindblom, B. (1992). Linguistic experience alters phonetic perception in infants by 6 months of age. *Science, 255,* 606–608.

Leach, P. (1995). *Prime Time Live*, ABC News.

Learning to read and write: Developmentally appropriate practices for young children. (1998). *Young Children, 53*(4), 30–46.

Levine, M. (2003). Getting at getting it: The quest for comprehension. *All Kinds of Minds* [On-line]. Available: http://www.allkindsofminds.org.

Levy, B. A., Abello, B., & Lysynchuk, L. (1997). Transfer from word training to reading in context: Gains in reading fluency and comprehension. *Learning Disability Quarterly, 20,* 173–188.

Liberman, I., Shankweiler, D., & Liberman, A. M. (1999). The alphabetic principle and learning to read. *Read all about it!* (pp. 117–130). Sacramento: California State Board of Education.

Lindamood, P., Bell, N., & Lindamood, P. (1997). Sensory-cognitive factors in the controversy over reading instruction. *Journal of Developmental and Learning Disorder, 1*(1), 143–182.

Linquanti, R. (1999). Fostering academic success for English language learners. What do we know? *WestEd* [On-line]. Available: http://www.wested.org/policy/pubs/fostering/misconceptions.htm.

Locke, J. (1994). Phases in a child's development of language. *American Scientist, 82,* 436–445.

Luce, P. (2002). Untitled presentation at the AASA annual meeting in Boston. Reported in *Brainwork, 12,* 2.

Lundberg, I., Olofsson, A., & Wall, S. (1980). Reading and spelling skills in the first school years predicted from phonemic awareness skills in kindergarten. *Scandinavian Journal of Psychology, 27,* 159–173.

Lyon, G. R. (2001, March 8). *Measuring success: Using assessments and accountability to raise student achievement.* Statement for the Subcommittee on Education Reform, Committee on Education and the Workforce, U.S. House of Representatives, Washington, DC. Retrieved February 20, 2003, from www.plato.com/pdf/teleconference_session3_lyon1.pdf.

Lyon, G. R. (2002). Why can't I read? *Northwest Education Magazine* [On-line], *8*(3). Available: http://www.nwrel.org/nwedu/08-03/read.asp.

Lyon, R. (2003). Presentation at the International Reading Association, Orlando, FL. Retrieved May 5, 2003, from www.reading.org/meetings/conv/conv03.news2. html.

Lyon, R., & Fletcher, J. M. (2001). Early warning systems. *Education Matters* [On-line]. Retrieved June 6, 2001, from www.edmatters.org/20012/22.html.

MacDonal, S. (1997). *The portfolio and its use: A road map for assessment.* Little Rock, AR: Southern Early Childhood Association.

Maclean, M., Bryant, P., & Bradley, L. (1978). Rhymes, nursery rhymes, and reading in early childhood. *Merrill-Palmer Quarterly, 33,* 255–281.

Mathes, P. (2003). *The Tallahassee and Houston first grade intervention studies.* Presentation at the International Reading Association, Orlando, FL.

McCracken, R. A. (1971). Initiating sustained silent reading. *Journal of Reading, 14*(8), 521–524, 582–583.

McEwan, E. K. (2002). *Teach them all to read: Catching the kids who fall through the cracks.* Thousand Oaks, CA: Corwin Press.

McGee, M. G., & Wilson, D. W. (1984). *Psychology: Science and application.* New York: West.

McPike, E. (1998). The unique power of reading and how to unleash it. *American Educator, 22*(1–2), 4–5.

Mehler, J., & Christophe, A. (1994). Language in the infant's mind. *Philosophical Transactions of the Royal Society (Biological Sciences), 346,* 13–20.

Meltzoff, A. N., & Moore, M. K. (1977). Imitation of facial and manual gestures by human neonates. *Science, 198,* 75–78.

Merzenich, M. M., Jenkins, W. M., Johnston, P., Schreiner, C., Miller, S. L., & Tallal, P. (1996). Temporal processing deficits of language-learning impaired children ameliorated by training. *Science, 271,* 77–81.

Meyer, R. J. (2003). Captives of the script: Killing us softly with phonics, a critical analysis demonstrates that scripted phonics programs hold students and teachers as curriculum hostages. *Rethinking Schools Online* [On-line], *17*(4). Available: http://www.rethinkingschools.org/archive/17_04/17_04.shtml.

Moats, L. C. (1998). Teaching decoding. *American Educator, 22*(1–2), 42–49, 95, 96.

Moats, L. C. (2001). *Speech to print: Language essentials for teachers.* Baltimore: Brookes Publishing.

Moats, L. C., Furry, A. R., & Brownell, N. (1998). *Learning to read: Components of beginning reading instruction, K–8.* Sacramento: Sacramento County Office of Education.

Morais, J., Bertelson, P., Cary, L., & Alegria, J. (1986). Literacy training and speech segmentation. *Cognition, 24,* 45–64.

National Association for the Education of Young Children. (1998). *Learning to read and write: Developmentally appropriate practices for young children.* A joint position statement of the International Reading Association and the National Association for the Education of Young Children, *53*(4), 30–46.

National Center for Education Statistics. (1998). *Digest of education statistics.* Washington, DC: U.S. Department of Education, Office of Educational Research and Improvement.

National Institute of Child Health and Human Development. (1998).

National Institute of Child Health and Human Development. (2002). Available: http://156.40.88.3/publications/pubs/readbro.htm.

National Reading Panel. (1999). *Teaching children to read: An evidence-based assessment of the scientific research literature on reading and its implications for reading instruction* [On-line]. Available: www.nationalreadingpanel.org/Publications/publications. htm.

Neuman, S. B. (2001). Access to print: Problem, consequences and instructional solutions. Address to the White House Summit on Early Childhood Cognitive Development. Washington, DC: U.S. Department of Education.

Neville, H. J. (1995). Developmental specificity in neurocognitive development in humans. In M. Gazzaniga (Ed.), *The cognitive neurosciences* (pp. 219–231). Cambridge, MA: MIT Press.

New York State Department, Office of Bilingual Education. (2000). *The teaching of language arts to limited English proficient/English language learners: A resource guide for all teachers.* Albany, NY: Author.

Nolte, J. (2002). *The human brain: An introduction to its functional anatomy* (5th ed.). St. Louis: Mosby.

Ogle, D. M. (1986). K-W-L: A teaching model that develops active reading of expository text. *The Reading Teacher, 40,* 564–570.

Oregon State Department of Education. (2003). *English/language arts grade level standards.* Portland, OR: Author.

Ortiz, A. (2001). English language learners with special needs: Effective instructional strategies. *ERIC Digest* [On-line], December, EDO- FL-01-08. Available: http://www.ericfacility.net/databases/ERIC_Digests/ed469207.html.

Paglin, C. (2002). *Double dose* [On-line]. Available: http://www.nwrel.org/nwedu/08-03/dose-t.asp.

Pascual-Leone, J. (1970). A maturational model for the transition rule in Piaget's developmental stages. *Acta Psychologica, 32,* 301–345.

Pennington, B. F. (1989). Using genetics to understand dyslexia. *Annals of Dyslexia, 39,* 81–93.

Perfetti, C. (1995). Cognitive research can inform reading education. *Journal of Research in Reading, 18,* 106–115.

Phillips, D. A., McCartney, K., & Scarr, S. (1987). Child-care quality and children's social development. *Developmental Psychology, 23,* 537–543.

Pianta, R. C. (1990). Widening the debate on educational reform: Prevention as a viable alternative. *Exceptional Children, 56*(4), 306–313.

Pilgreen, J. (2000). *Using sustained silent reading to develop students' comprehension and motivation to read.* Presentation at the Secondary Schools Reading Summit, San Bernardino County Superintendent of Schools.

Pinker, S. (1997). *How the mind works.* New York: W. W. Norton.

Pressley, M. (1998). *Reading instruction that works: The case for balanced teaching.* New York: Guilford Press.

Pressley, M. (2001). Comprehension instruction: What makes sense now, what might make sense soon. *Reading Online* [On-line], 5(2). Available: http://www.readingonline.org/articles/art_index.asp?HREF=/articles/handbook/pressley/Index.html.

Purcell-Gates, V., & Dahl, K. (1991). Low-SES children's success and failure at early literacy learning in skills-based classrooms. *JRB: A Journal of Literacy, 23,* 1–34.

Rasinski, T. (2000). Speed does matter in reading. *The Reading Teacher, 54*(2), 146–151.

Rayner, K., Foorman, B. R., Perfetti, C. A., Pesetsky, D., & Seidenberg, M. S. (2002). How should reading be taught? *Scientific American, 286*(3), 70–77.

Restak, R. (2001). *The secret life of the brain.* Washington, DC: Joseph Henry Press.

Road to Reading (1997). *Emerging literacy* [On-line]. Available: http://www.ed.gov/pubs/RoadtoRead/part2.html.

Scarborough, H. S. (1989). Prediction of reading disability from familial and individual differences. *Journal of Educational Psychology, 81*(1), 101–108.

Shaywitz, S. (2003). *Overcoming dyslexia: A new and complete science-based program for reading problems at any level.* New York: Alfred A Knopf.

Shaywitz, S. E., Fletcher, J. M., & Shaywitz, B. A. (1994). Issues in the definition and classification of attention deficit disorder. *Topics in Language Disorders, 14*(4), 1–25.

Shaywitz, S. E., & Shaywitz, B. A. (2001). The neurobiology of reading and dyslexia. *Focus on Basics, 5*(A).

Shaywitz, B. A., Shaywitz, S. E., Pugh, K. R., Mencl, W. E., Fulbright, R. K., Skudlarski, P., Constable, R. T., Marchione, K. E., Fletcher, J. M., Lyon, G. R., & Gore, J. C. (2002). Functional disruption in the organization of the brain for reading in dyslexia. *Biological Psychiatry, 52,* 101–110.

Sherman, L. (2002). Why can't I read? Current research offers new hope to disabled learners. *Northwest Education Magazine* [On-line]. Available: www.nwrel.org/nwedu/08-03/read.asp.

Slavin, R. E. (1994). *Preventing early school failure: Research, policy, and practice.* Needham Heights, MA: Longwood Division, Allyn & Bacon.

Slavin, R. E., & Madden, N. (1994). *Effects of success for all on the achievement of English language learners.* Paper presented at the annual meeting of the American Educational Research Association, San Francisco.

Smith, F. (1998). *The book of learning and forgetting.* New York: Teachers College Press.

Snow, C. E., Burns, M. S., & Griffin, P. (1998). *Preventing reading difficulties in young children.* Washington, DC: National Academy Press.

Snow, C. E., & Tabors, P. O. (1993). Language skills that relate to literacy development. In B. Spodek & O. N. Saracho (Eds.), *Language and literacy in early childhood education.* New York: Teachers College Press.

Southern California Comprehensive Assistance Center. (2002). *Taking a reading: A teacher's guide to reading assessment.* Downey, CA: Los Angeles County Office of Education.

Stahl, S. A. (1999). *Vocabulary development, from reading research to practice: A series for teachers.* Newton Upper Falls, MA: Brookline Books.

Stahl, S. A. (2003, Spring). How words are learned incrementally over multiple exposures. *American Educator, 18–19.*

Stanovich, K. E. (1986). Matthew effects in reading: Some consequences of individual differences in the acquisition of literacy. *Reading Research Quarterly, 21,* 360–407.

Stanovich, K. E. (1988). Explaining the differences between the dyslexic and the garden-variety poor reader: The phonological-core variable-difference model. *Journal of Learning Disabilities, 21,* 590–612.

Stanovich, K. E., Cunningham, A. E., & Cramer, B. B. (1984). Assessing phonological awareness in kindergarten children: Issues of task comparability. *Journal of Experimental Child Psychology, 38,* 175–190.

Sylwester, R. (1995). *A celebration of neurons: An educator's guide to the human brain.* Alexandria, VA: Association for Supervision and Curriculum Development.

Sylwester, R. (1998). Art for the brain's sake. *Educational Leadership, 5*(3), 31–35.

Tallal, P. (2000). Experimental studies of language learning impairments: From research to remediation. In D. V. M. Bishop & L. B. Leonard (Eds.), *Speech and language impairments in children: Causes, characteristics, intervention, and outcome.* Hove, UK: Psychology Press.

Teale, W. H. (1984). Reading to young children: Its significance for literacy development. In H. Goelman, A. Oberg, & F. Smith (Eds.), *Awakening to literacy.* Portsmouth, NH: Heinemann.

Teale, W. H. (1988). Emergent literacy as a perspective for examining how young children become readers and writers. *Emergent Literacy,* Norwood, NJ: Ablex Publishing.

Teale, W. H., & Sulzby, E. (1986). Emergent literacy as a perspective for examining how young children become readers and writers. In W. H. Teale & E. Sulzby (Eds.), *Emergent literacy: Reading and writing.* Norwood, NJ: Ablex Publishing.

Temple, E., Deutsch, G. K., Poldrac, R. A., Salidis, J., Deutsch, G. K., Miller, S. L., Tallal, P., Merzenich, M. M., & Gabrieli, J. D. (2003). Neural deficits in children with dyslexia ameliorated by behavioral remediation: Evidence from functional MRI. *Proceedings of the National Academy of Science, 100*(5), 2860–2865.

Templeton, S., & Morris, D. (1999). Questions teachers ask about spelling. *Reading Research Quarterly, 34*(1), 102–112.

Texas Assessment of Academic Skills. (1997). *Texas essential knowledge and skills for English language arts and reading* [On-line]. Available: www.tea.state.tx.us/teks/teksls.pdf.

Torgesen, J. K. (1993). Variations on theory in learning disability. In G. R. Lyon, D. B. Gray, J. E. Kavanagh, & N. A. Krasnegor (Eds.), *Better understanding of learning disabilities: New views from research and their implications for education and public policies* (pp. 153–170). Baltimore: Brookes Publishing.

Torgesen, J. (1998). Catch them before they fall: Identification and assessment to prevent reading failure in young children. *American Educator, 22*(1–2), 32–39.

Torgesen, J. K., & Burgess, S. R. (1998). Consistency of reading-related phonological processes throughout early childhood: Evidence from longitudinal-correlational and instructional studies. In J. Tetsala & L. Ehri (Eds.), *Word recognition in beginning reading.* Hillsdale, NJ: Erlbaum.

Torgesen, J. K., Wagner, R. K., & Rashotte, C. A. (1994). Longitudinal studies of phonological processing and reading. *Journal of Learning Disabilities, 27,* 276–286.

Tracey, E. H. (1994). Family literacy: Research synthesis. Paper presented at the Annual Meeting of the National Reading Conference, San Diego.

Tuma, R. S. (2002). How do we remember? Let us count the ways. *Brain Work, The Neuroscience Newsletter, 12*(6), 1–2.

Tunmer, W. E., Herriman, M. L., & Nesdale, A. R. (1988). Metalinguistic abilities and beginning reading. *Reading Research Quarterly, 23,* 134–158.

Vaughn, S., Hughes, M. T., Moody, S. W., & Elbaum, B. (2001). Instructional grouping for reading for students with LD: Implications for practice. *Intervention in School and Clinic, 36*(3), 131–137.

Viadero, D. (2002). Studies back lessons in writing, spelling. *Education Week* [On-line]. Available: www.edweek.org.

Vukelich, C., Christie, J., & Enz, B. (2002). *Helping young children learn language and literacy.* Boston: Allyn & Bacon.

Walsh, D. J., Price, G. G., & Gillingham, M. G. (1988). The critical but transitory importance of letter naming. *Reading Research Quarterly, 23,* 108–122.

Walsh, K. (2003). Basal readers: The lost opportunity to build the knowledge that propels comprehension. *American Educator, 27*(1), 24–27.

Wells, G. (1985). *The meaning makers.* Portsmouth, NH: Heinemann.

Whitehurst, G. J., Falco, F., Lonigan, C. J., Fischal, J. E., DeBaryshe, B. D., Valdez-Manchaca, M. C., & Caulfield, M. (1988). Accelerating language development through picturebook reading. *Developmental Psychology, 24,* 552–559.

Wolf, M. (2003). Teaching fluency with Maryanne Wolf, new research on an old problem: A brief history of fluency. *Scholastic* [On-line]. Available: www.teacher.scholastic.com/reading/bestpractices/index.htm.

Wolf, M., Bowers, P., & Biddle, K. (2000). RAVE-O: A comprehensive fluency-based reading intervention program. *Journal of Learning Disabilities, 33*(4).

Wolfe, P. (2001). *Brain matters: Translating research into classroom practice.* Alexandria, VA: Association for Supervision and Curriculum Development.

Yopp, H. K. (1985). Read-aloud books for developing phonemic awareness: An annotated bibliography. *Reading Teacher, 48,* 538–542.

Index

**CORWIN
PRESS**

The Corwin Press logo—a raven striding across an open book—represents the union of courage and learning. Corwin Press is committed to improving education for all learners by publishing books and other professional development resources for those serving the field of K–12 education. By providing practical, hands-on materials, Corwin Press continues to carry out the promise of its motto: **"Helping Educators Do Their Work Better."**